Nature of Compa

A Philosophical Analysis

Nature of Compassion

A Philosophical Analysis

Kirandeep Kaur

ADROIT

Adroit Publishers

New Delhi

ISBN : 978-81-87393-53-5

First Published in 2017

Published by
ADROIT PUBLISHERS
4675/21, Ganpati Bhawan, Ansari Road,
Daryaganj, New Delhi-110 002
Phone : 011-23266030

Exclusively Distributed by:

Vijay Enterprises
4675/21, Ganpati Bhawan,
Ansari Road, Daryaganj
New Delhi, INDIA
Mob.: +91-9899717865

Typesetting—Gaurav Graphices, Delhi-110002
E-mail: gauravsingh1908@gmail.com
Printed at: Rajyoriya Prints, Delhi.

जतु सतु चावल दइआ कणक करि प्रापति पाती धानु।
दूधु करमु सतोखु घीउ करि ऐसा मॉगउ दानु।।

"Please bless me with the rice of truth and self-restraint, the wheat of compassion, and the leaf-plate of meditation. Bless me with the milk of good karma, and the clarified butter, the ghee, of compassion. Such are the gifts I beg of you, lord."[1]

Acknowledgements

My sincere thanks to my revered supervisor Dr. Pragati Sahni for her support, guidance and encouragement throughout this work. I deeply appreciate her contribution of time and ideas. I also thank all other faculty members and all my friends who guided me through the process and never accepting less than my best efforts.

It would be unfair on my part if I do not thank my mother who helped me with many things and gave me the much needed boost from time to time. I would like to thanks to every source that made this thesis possible.

Contents

	Acknowledgements	*vii*
	Introduction	1
1.	Compassion: A General Introduction	9
2.	Nature of Compassion; Aristotle, Aquinas and Nussbaum	22
3.	Nature of Compassion: Buddhism and Sikhism	49
4.	Conclusion	80
	Bibliography	88
	References	92
	Index	107

Introduction

The present research work entitled: "Nature of Compassion; A Philosophical Analysis", aims to discern the nature of compassion through the comparative study of some Western and Indian philosophical traditions.

Compassion can be considered as one cornerstone of greater social interconnection and humanity in society. Human beings exist within relationships. They are born dependent. Right from the very birth, they need protection and care. As they grow up they require relationships with others for their survival (e.g., food, shelter and reproduction). Generally speaking, compassion is regarded as helping human beings function in these relationships with greater harmony, hence further contributing to their survival. And not merely to survival, it even to an extent underlies law and order in society.

Compassion has been a matter of considerable importance ever since the faculty of thought in humans developed. It is argued that the human species could not have survived if egocentric living were the basis of human interactions. Compassion has been a central focus of many religions and ethical traditions, from Buddhism to Christianity. For example, Buddhists view compassion as central to liberating our minds from the power of destructive emotions such as fear, anger, envy, and vengeance. They teach compassion as an antidote to cruelty.[2] Sikhism contends that the path of righteousness can be found only by practicing compassion.[3] The

Biblical tradition too holds compassion as "a duty to divine law, as a response to divine love, and a sign of commitment to the Judeo-Christian ethics."[4] Many conversations can be easily found on compassion in and across religion, philosophy, psychology, sociology and medicine dating back two and a half thousand years and more. The present research however intends to analyze compassion philosophically. Even in the domain of philosophy, it is not an untouched discourse. Many philosophers view compassion as the cornerstone of morality, e.g., Schopenhauer postulates it as central to morality[5] and Nussbaum sees it as a source of principled moral judgment.[6]

The word compassion is commonly used and referred to by people to describe their altruistic feelings or concern for others' suffering without really knowing the nature of it. Most of us would doubtlessly agree that news of the terrorists' attacks on innocents, stories of rape victims, sights of terrible road accidents, and viewing starving people incites our compassion.[7] Humans, as social animals, seem to feel compassion towards a wide variety of objects in a wide range of situations. But there is nothing clear about this word except that it implies a feeling in the subject towards the suffering of the victim or sufferer. The history of philosophy offers multifarious definitions of the term: some suggest that compassion is connected to pain or sorrow (Aristotle)[8]; some suggest it is not (Buddhists)[9]; some say that it requires the blamelessness of the sufferer for his/her suffering (Nussbaum)[10]; and others that it is simply a complex emotional attitude toward another (Blum)[11]. But the presence of these different philosophical views makes it difficult for us to come to a consensus on what the nature of the term is.

As we know compassion is aroused by the sight of suffering. That's why many believe that compassion is closely related to the experience of sorrow and pain. But the nature of this sorrow or pain is not clear. It is debatable whether sorrow or pain of the compassion-feeler is same as the sufferer himself or is different? That is, 'whether my pain or sorrow is same as the physical pain my friend is suffering because of her broken leg; or it is a kind of psychological pain?' The second problem is; 'whether compassion is only a response towards serious suffering or is it a sympathetic response even towards non-serious suffering?' The next complexity comes with the question: who will judge the 'seriousness of suffering' (the compassion-feeler or the sufferer?). It is also a puzzle whether compassion involves co-suffering or not. Compassion, as the etymology of the term (*co-suffering*) suggests, can be felt towards those who are aware of their suffering (as maintained by Brain Carr).[12] But, Nussbaum, on this argues that to feel compassion it is not necessary that the sufferer be aware of his condition.[13]

Yet another position says that in order to know the suffering of another being, one needs to stand in direct relation to that being (sufferer). Compassion always exists in a dyadic relationship, i.e., between a subject (compassion-feeler) and the sufferer, but it is unclear and ambiguous on just how this relationship is formed (and on what factors it depends)? Most philosophical accounts of compassion rely on the idea that this relationship can be achieved through imaginative dwelling on the other's condition.[14] While some other philosophers believe that compassion is not an abstract extrapolation of what one assumes to be the nature of the victim's suffering, but is rather the shared experience of suffering with the victim.[15] There are still others who maintain that particular sets of beliefs about one's own vulnerabilities and consequent liabilities to misfortune make it possible for a compassionate-feeler to make a relation with a sufferer.[16] Because of such diverse views, there is no consensus about this relationship.

Another ambiguous question is whether compassion is actually one of our morally based emotions comparable to notions like pity, or it is a social virtue? It is another puzzle to try and figure out whether the ability to feel compassion towards the unfortunate represents a human instinct, or is it something learnt through practice? Many philosophers in different stages of time worked hard to find an answer. As a result we are confronted with many different views. And because of numerous views many uncertainties still continue to exist in this notion.

Thus the central aim of this work is to determine the nature of compassion by analyzing its conceptual structure and the following set of questions, which I found are necessary to understand the nature of compassion to full capacity.

- Is compassion the same as or distinct from pity, sympathy/empathy, love, and benevolence?
- Does compassion involve sorrow or pain?
    - If it involves suffering, then what kind of suffering is this?
    - Does the compassionate subject suffer with same intensity sufferer himself suffers?
- Is compassion only a response towards serious suffering, or it is also a response towards non-serious suffering?
- How does the compassionate subject make a relationship with the sufferer?
- Is compassion a virtue or an emotion?
- Is compassion a part of human instinct or is it learnt through practice?
- Is there or can there be one universal understanding of the term compassion?

In this study thus I will take up these issues in part or in full to unravel the nature of compassion. My account of compassion is a comparative study of Western (Aristotle, Aquinas and Nussbaum) and Indian schools of thought (Buddhism and Sikhism).

Method

The present is a philosophical study on many works, primarily of ethics and religion. For this study I read primary and secondary texts concerning ethics and religion. This study is grounded on some religious texts, yet it will not be a theological study based simply on religious faith and discourse. In other words, this research is mostly philosophical and not religious or historical in the sense of the appreciation of any religious teaching during any particular period.

The scope of this study is intentionally wide in the sense that it covers the work of many philosophers. In terms of time, it extends over a period of nearly three thousand years, from 3rd century B.C.E. to the 21st century, yet the research can be regarded as limited and focused because it is only concerned with one philosophical issue, i.e., the nature of compassion.

Literature Review

Before moving further, it will be valuable to look at the work of other scholars on compassion. Many works exists that discuss compassion. But most of them have little to say on the nature of compassion. They talk about its role in our moral world. It is commonly believed to be an ethical notion. Below is an account of some of the noteworthy works on compassion.

One important work in this field is by Lawrence Blum. Blum, in his paper 'Compassion' claims that compassion is a moral phenomenon. He demonstrates that it is a motive to beneficence, which has strength, stability and reliability.[17] Here his views are influenced by Arthur Schopenhauer's critique of Kant's ethics. In *On the Basis of Morality*, Schopenhauer maintains that compassion is central to morality, i.e., only those actions which spring from compassion have moral values, and other actions which result from any other motives have none.[18] In addition, C. Taylor in 'Sympathy' observes that our sympathetic responses, our immediate and unthinking, cannot be explained in terms of some fundamental features of human existence.[19]

Further, in order to understand the Theravāda Buddhist concept of compassion, I find Harvey Aronson's book *Love and Sympathy in Theravāda Buddhism* to be very helpful.[20] The book discusses the context and content of the Theravāda teachings on *brahmavihāra* (set of four sublime attitudes), universal love, compassion, sympathetic joy and equanimity. Chapter one and two gives a detailed account of compassion, as mentioned in the earliest of Theravāda scripture complied before 350 B.C.E. Here Aronson's concern is not only the description of Pāli material relevant to these topics, but also with the motives to social action as well as the psychological and soteriological import of the Theravāda teaching on the sublime attitudes (i.e., universal love, compassion, etc.).

Another significant work in this field is Chris Frakers' paper 'Do the Compassionate Flourish? Overcoming Anguish and Impulse towards Violence'. In this paper, he argues that in order for compassion to be considered a virtue, Western philosophical accounts of compassion must be supplemented by Buddhist understandings. He finds that the Western concept of compassion has two potential problems, that is, it may burden the compassionate agent with anguish such that he cannot flourish and that feeling compassion may give rise to violence on behalf of the suffering. Besides these problems, he also discusses how the proper emotion which demonstrates the virtue of compassion is that of equanimity. Another book called *An Introduction to Buddhist Ethics*, written by Peter Harvey, also brings out an analysis of the nature and practical dynamics of various notions of Buddhist ethics.[21] Harvey brings to light compassion as one of the key Buddhist values, which is important for inter-personal and social relationships.

In Sikh literature there is no work as such which deals solely with the nature of compassion. Although its essence can be seen in the Ādi Granth and Janam Sākhis, it is yet still a raw subject-matter to be dealt with philosophically. One small section is devoted by Satnaạm Kaur in her book *Three Basics of Sikh Religious Thought* on compassion as a quality of God, (however not on the nature of compassion).[22] The presentation of her work is based on the teachings of ***Guru Granth Sahib***, where compassion is described as one of the attributes of God, as God's force, which sustains and permeates whatever is present in the world. In addition to Satnaam Kaur's book, Avtar Singh's book *Ethics of the Sikhs*, offers a rigorous philosophical discussion of Sikh ethics. His work shows a systematic study of the authentic ethical speculations in Sikhism. Although in this work, compassion is not discussed directly, it is an important source to understand the basic tenets of ethics in Sikhism.

The above discussion includes only a small section of original and scholarly work on compassion. I will use these and other works in order to build up an understanding of compassion that may be clearer and more appealing universally.

Structure of the Research

My research is organized into four chapters. The first chapter focuses on a general understanding of compassion. For this purpose, I start with an explanation of its etymological meaning and move on to the dictionary meaning to explain how is it different from what is generally taken to be its synonyms such as pity, sympathy and love. This discussion further discusses the relationship between the compassionate subject and the sufferer.

The second chapter covers the Western and contemporary concept of compassion. To get a wider and a better picture of the concept, I have chosen three philosophers from three different time-periods: first from the early Greeks, namely Aristotle, second from the medieval period, namely St. Aquinas, and third from the contemporary period, namely Martha Nussbaum. A section each is devoted to each thinker. Here, for the sake of practicability, I intend to focus my concern on two things: first, is the impartial explanation of compassion as defined by these philosophers; second, an analysis of the set of questions raised in the introduction.

The third chapter analyzes the nature of compassion in the Eastern framework. For this purpose I have chosen the philosophies of two different schools: Buddhism and Sikhism, which as we know, exist with the same intensity as in the past. The first section explores the views of early Buddhism on compassion, and the second section covers the view of Sikhism on compassion. To understand the nature of compassion better, I also go on to find answers to the various questions raised in the introduction, as I did in the last chapter. In the third section of this chapter I analyze discussions of contemporary writers and also try to find the best possible answer that could well go with Buddhism and Sikhism.

My fourth and final chapter analyses and shares my findings. I hope that further research will benefit from my study especially that which proposes to look into the meaning and nature of compassion as presented in various Western and Indian schools of thought.

1

Compassion: A General Introduction

The word compassion immediately leads our minds to examples such as when an old woman unable to cross the road, is helped by a young man moved by her condition.[23]

Compassion, in common usage, refers to a deep awareness of the suffering of another, coupled with the wish to heal it. It is generally believed that acts of compassion are encouraged by moral systems around the compassion-feeler's world, and include the feeling of mercy, gentleness, tenderness, generosity, kindness, patience, and self-sacrifice or altruistic behavior. The word, compassion has its own etymological history. The English noun compassion, meaning to suffer together with, comes from the Latin. Its prefix *com-* comes directly from *com*, an archaic version of the Latin preposition and affix *cum* (that means with); the *passion* segment is derived from *passus*, past participle of the deponent verb *patior, patî, passus sum*. Compassion is thus related in origin, form and meaning to the English noun *patient* (meaning one who suffers), which comes from *patiens*, the present participle of the same *patior*, and is akin to the Greek verb *paskhein*, taken to mean to suffer, and to its cognate noun *pathos.*[24] Despite this the exact nature of the term is not clear. Thus compassion, because of its puzzling nature, has long been a playing field upon which many philosophers have silently battled. Some say it is the same as 'pity,' whilst others say that it is same as 'sympathy' or 'empathy'. Some even argue that it is identical with the feeling of 'love'.

To analyze it better, let us look at the definitions given by the Oxford Dictionary:[25]

(1) Suffering together with another, participation in suffering; fellow-feeling, *sympathy*.[26]

(2) *Pity*[27]; that inclines one to spare or to succor.

(3) The feeling or emotion, when a person is moved by the suffering or distress of another, and by the desire to relieve it.

These three corresponding definitions, I feel, raise some serious questions – "Does compassion only mean to feel pity or sympathy on others' plight?" or "Are they interchangeable terms?" Let us analyze them individually.

Many mistake compassion as the same as sympathy, as the two share some common features. Sympathy and compassion are both feelings which are focused on the object. In Nancy E. Snow's words both are "other-regarding" emotions,[28] i.e., both feelings focus on the object rather than the owner of these feelings. The second similarity between both feelings is, as Snow,[29] Gregory Pence,[30] Brain Carr,[31] and many more maintain, that these both are aroused by negative conditions (like suffering, pain, etc.) of the object. Third, in both feelings the perception of the negative condition of the object in question evokes sorrow and suffering in the subject. But besides all these similarities, both terms have a different and independent identity.

In order to understand the difference between these two terms, first it is important to understand what sympathy is. The Oxford dictionary uses the term sympathy while defining compassion. And the same (Oxford) dictionary defines sympathy as: "sharing the feelings of others (especially feelings of sorrow or anguish)." This implies that it is only a fellow-feeling with the sufferer. When someone sympathizes with the other, he/she is inclined to believe that what the other is undergoing is bad. It does not necessarily incline one to make a wish for or show concern for the others' well-being. The sympathy-feeler may or may not be concerned with the well-being of the one who is suffering. In simpler words, the feeling of sympathy in someone's heart does not bind him to make a wish or desire of healing the others' plight. On the other hand, the feeling of compassion, by its very definition, is bound to a wish or desire to alleviate suffering. The other difference between sympathy and compassion is that sympathy can be directed to classes of persons (e.g., the persons with disability) or to general conditions of poverty,[32] while the feeling of compassion is always directed towards a particular person.

Further, as Snow[33] and Lawrence Blum[34] maintain, sympathy differs from compassion in being an appropriate response to a wider range of misfortunes, including those less serious. In simpler words, sympathy has a wider range than compassion. For example, one can feel sympathy for a person's irritation, discomfort, inconvenience, or displeasure. That is, one might sympathize with someone whose favorite pen has been lost or whose car has been scratched, but one would not ordinarily feel compassionate for that person.[35] In this manner, sympathy differs from compassion because sympathy is often a less intense emotional reaction than is compassion. People feel more compassionate toward those peoples by whose conditions they usually get more deeply affected. In Snow's words, 'The more deeply we are moved by the other's plight, the more intense is our emotional response.'[36] This last difference leads to a further debatable question: 'Is compassion only a response towards serious misfortune or is it a response even towards a less serious ones?' I will discuss this question later in this paper. Thus, here, I conclude from first two differences. From the above, it can be gathered that compassion includes the feeling of sympathy, as compassion like sympathy is a response to the others' plight. But both terms are not synonyms or interchangeable terms.

Now, while comparing compassion with pity, many maintain that pity and compassion share the same emotional landscape.[37] Pity has some resemblance with compassion, since it also arises from the suffering of others, but it is not totally the same as the feeling of compassion. There is a finite line which distinguishes pity from compassion. Before proceeding any further, it is important to know what pity is. The Oxford dictionary defines pity as: 'a feeling of sympathy and sorrow for the misfortunes of others'. From this definition it looks as if the feeling of pity is very much similar to the feeling of compassion, because both feelings involve sympathy and sorrow[38] for the sufferer. But, there is an urgency or immediacy about compassion that pity lacks, as maintained by Snow.[39] For Pence, the word pity, unlike compassion, includes condescension and interpersonal distance from the object of emotion.[40] We can understand this point in the following manner. When one pities another, one feels sorry for that person but at the same time he or she maintains a distance from that person. Many contemporary philosophers hold that this distance exists either because the subject believes that he himself is not vulnerable, i.e., in future, he or she would not experience the same negative conditions as the one whom they pity, or because he believes that the sufferer brings suffering on himself. In simpler words, in pity, in contrast to compassion, one finds unfortunate the object of pity, and also believes that he himself is not and would not be unfortunate in a similar way. According to Snow, the hallmark of pity is the denial that those who feel it could experience another's misfortune or could experience it in the same degrading or humiliating way.[41] The second feature which distinguishes both from one another is 'the condition of blame-worthiness.'[42] Many maintain that we generally don't feel compassionate for those people whom we consider guilty. In other words, if we know that the sufferer (object of pity) is responsible for his suffering then we don't feel compassionate towards him, but at the same time we might feel pity for his condition per se. For example, one might feel pity for the bad condition of an imprisoned thief. But one would not feel compassion for his condition. Because one assumes that he brings suffering on himself, i.e., he is responsible for his condition. As Blum wrote, 'sometimes the reason we feel pity rather than compassion is that we feel that the object has in some way brought the suffering on himself or deserved it, or in any case that he allowed himself to be humiliated or degraded by it.'[43] On this point, Snow also agrees with Blum. Snow suggests that these above two features allow the subject (pity-feeler) to maintain a sense of superiority towards the pity-object.[44] The points made here are debatable, which I will discuss, in detail, in later chapters.

Carr points out that compassion can be felt only in the case of felt suffering.[45] According to him there are two kinds of sufferings: felt suffering and unfelt suffering.[46] Felt suffering is that in which the sufferer is aware of his suffering. And, in unfelt suffering, the sufferer is not aware of his condition. For example, a financial loss which I suffer but which I am unaware of; or the death of a distant relative which never comes to my attention; or a permanent comatose state which I suffering.[47] And as the etymology of the word compassion suggests, compassion means 'suffering with', it (compassion) cannot be experienced when the sufferer himself is not feeling anything. Suppose a cancer patient is in coma and he is not in a state to feel pain. Then in this case one cannot feel with the sufferer. Thus, rather than being compassionate, the subjects feels pity for the object (sufferer).

From the above discussion, it can be said that pity is different from compassion, because pity includes a stance of superiority towards the object of feeling, which compassion lacks. And the feeling of condescension and superiority exists only when the subject is some distance from the sufferer. And, moreover, pity, like sympathy, is not linked with the concern of the sufferer's well-being. Thus the meaning of compassion is over and above that of the meaning of sympathy and pity. Compassion is "suffering with another" that includes an altruistic concern for the other's good. Pity is a more spectator-like[48] feeling, according to which we can pity someone while maintaining a safe emotional distance from what the sufferer is undergoing. When we feel compassion, as Snow maintains, this emotional distance is crossed, and we desire to relieve the other's plight.[49] Thus, the pivot of compassion is one's ability to feel with the sufferer, which makes the other's suffering real to those who feel compassionate, and facilitates good-hearted desires for the other's good as maintained by both Snow and Blum.[50]

Sometimes the feeling of compassion is confused with the feeling of benevolence and love. The feeling of benevolence is not same as compassion, as it (benevolence) carries a much broader meaning than does compassion. Benevolence is the desire to do good for others and isn't necessarily focused on suffering. Compassion contains within it benevolence but benevolence does not necessarily contain compassion. Love is also not a synonym for compassion. Both feelings appear synonymic to each other because both include active concern for the other's good. But both are different by their very definition. To analyze on what ground both are different, first it is important to clarify the definition of love. The English word 'Love' is an abstract word, because it refers to a variety of different feelings, states, and attitudes, ranging from pleasure ("I loved that meal") to interpersonal attraction ("I love my partner"). This diversity of uses and meanings makes love unusually difficult to consistently define. For the present purpose, we can stick to the meaning found in Oxford Dictionary: 'warm affection, attachment, affectionate devotion etc'. From this it follows that love is a powerful emotion involving an intense attachment to an object and a high evaluation of it. It is an active interest in the wellbeing of the object caused by affection for the object. Thus, in love, the subject-object relation is based on attachment and affection. On the other hand, in compassion it is not necessary that the subject is related with the object because of attachment or affection. In the following pages I am going to describe the relation between the compassionate-subject and the sufferer.

Nature and Types of the Relation Present Between Compassion-Feeler and Sufferer

Compassion, as stated above, is an altruistic behavior, which involves a shared feeling of suffering and also involves an intense desire to relieve the sufferer. Two persons can share the same feeling only when the two persons identify themselves with each other. Snow illustrates this point by saying that the '......philosophical account of compassion relies on the idea that it must be possible for those who feel compassion to identify with those with those for whom the emotion is felt'.[51]

There are three prevailing views among philosophers through which this identification or relation or link can be achieved. The first is imagination of object conditions, the second is recognition of our own vulnerability and the third is love. The first view is popular among philosophers like Blum and Pence; the second view is held by Aristotle and Snow; and the third one supported in Buddhism and Sikhism.

The possessors of the first view assert that identification between compassion-feeler (subject) and sufferer can be achieved through imaginative dwelling on the other's plight.[52] While the holders of the second view assert that this identification is affected by the beliefs held by subjects who are frequently victims of misfortune or suffering about their own similarities to the sufferer.[53] Let's analyze these views in detail:

> The possessors of the first view maintain that the *imagination* plays a key role in achieving understanding and feelings of suffering people. So primarily it becomes more important to understand first 'what is imagination?' There are three ways in which imagination can be understood. The first type of imagination involves complete *self-transposal* into another's situation.[54] The second type of imagination is based on the past memory of subject. And, the third is purely intellectual reconstruction of another's situation, by understanding of his values and belief systems.

According to the first type of imagination, the subject identifies with the other person. The subject thinks that he himself is a sufferer. Here generally identity confusion is involved, and because of this confusion the subject fails to distinguish his feelings and situation from the sufferer. As Blum expounds, 'such a pathological condition actually precludes genuine compassion because it blurs the distinction between subject and object.'[55]

In the second type of imagination, the subject makes an identity with the object because of having had an experience similar to the sufferer. Here, the subject's judgment is totally based on his past memories, which evokes his experience. In simpler words, the compassionate person identifies with the sufferer, because he himself had gone through the same situation. In this case identity confusion is not involved. But this type of imagination doesn't totally satisfy the need of compassion. As Blum writes, '....for compassion does not require even that its subject have experienced the sort of suffering that occasions it. We can commiserate with someone who has lost a child in a fire, even if we do not have a child or have never lost someone we love.'[56]

The third type of imagination involves intellectual imaginative reconstruction of the sufferer's situation. This imaginative reconstruction does not merely include the understanding of the sufferer's condition by imagining what our own reaction would be in that similar condition, it includes a richer and powerful imagination of the other's situation. In simple words, this one takes greater imagination and experience needed to understand it. Without a powerful and strong imagination, the understanding of others' suffering, not of one's own background, values or needs, is not possible. To emphasize this point, Blum writes, '......the imaginative reconstruction involved in compassion consists in imagining what the other person, given his character, beliefs and value is undergoing, rather than what we ourselves would feel in his situation.'[57] Pence also says that it is not enough to transpose one's own views unto the sufferer because 'selves' and personalities differ. That is people differ greatly in what they value and feel, what creates suffering differs among people.[58] To make this point more clear Pence quotes a famous saying of George Bernard Shaw: 'do not do unto others what you want done to you: their tastes might be different.' And if one does this then it will be a grave mistake. Pence further points out that the imagination required for ideal compassion is more than an imaginative self-transposal, i.e., more than a golden rule of putting oneself in the sufferer's place. To explain this further Blum offers an example; suppose a man (X), who might regard his son's decision to work for the CIA with distress, while someone (Y) with different beliefs and values might regard such a decision with pride: yet this other person may well be able to understand X's reaction and to feel compassion for X.[59] By referring this example, Carr writes, 'this case.......go[es] to the heart of the matter'.[60] He (Carr) further writes that in this case the onlooker (subject) is moved by the very real suffering which the father is going through and not by his personal judgment on the situation.[61] In simpler words, here the subject (onlooker) has achieved an insight into values and beliefs of suffering parents. He (onlooker) appreciates the father's predicament, given a set of values and beliefs in terms of which the decision is a major misfortune. In this sense, a strong and powerful imagination is needed to transcend our own personal judgment and understand the situation in terms of sufferer's heart and mind.

Pence maintains that this kind of understanding is an achievement. He asserts this, because, this understanding presupposes an intimacy between people through which the sufferer reveals personal details to the listener.[62] He further maintains that this kind of intimacy is built on related moral qualities between the listener and sufferer of trust, honesty, and time of willingness to listen.[63] Pence says 'such intimacy and understanding is not mundane, an easily generated moral phenomenon, but is instead a 'virtue' as Aristotle understood the term: an excellence manifesting the best in humans and their civilization.'[64]

The second way by which identity can be established is recognition of our-own vulnerability. This view is introduced by Aristotle. There are many philosophers including Snow who admired this view. According to Aristotle this is an important feature of compassion. He maintains that in order to feel compassion, we must obviously be capable of supposing that some evil may happen to us or some friend of ours, i.e., I myself am vulnerable in similar ways, as the others are. In simpler words, compassion is facilitated by the realization that we and those close to us can experience misfortune. Snow also asserts the same point by writing that 'our ability to identify with others is promoted by our belief that we are similar to them. Our ability to relate to them emotionally and to desire their good is promoted by caring for them......that is, our judgment that others are similar to us in various ways facilitates our ability to care about them and to express this concern emotionally.'[65] According to Snow, at the heart of this link is the belief that "it could be me."[66] Nussbaum extends this point by saying that a judgment of similar possibilities is an epistemological aid to forming the eudemonistic judgment, i.e., others are an important parts of one's own scheme of goals and projects, important as ends in their own right.[67]

Besides these two ways there is a third one, called love, by which a subject can establish an identity or link with compassionate-object. There are two ways in which love can be understood. First, as mentioned earlier love can be seen as a warm affection, attachment, affectionate devotion, as usually defined in contemporary world. This kind of love involves an intense attachment with few objects. In this form of love, a lover always seeks the active interest in the well-being of the object because of his attachment. Here, attachment enables the compassion-feeler to feel compassion for the sufferer. As Snow details in her article, 'love too can enable us to feel compassion for those we love even though we are unable to imagine their experiences.'[68] There are some cases in which the subject is not able to imagine the situation of the sufferer, for example in the case of a drug addict. It is possible that the addict's world could well be beyond the reach of our and his parents' imaginative abilities. But an addict's parents' love for their child could allow them to identify with his needs and wants, and thus be sufficient to motivate a compassionate response without aid of imagination.[69]

The second type of love is unconditional as described in the teaching of Buddhism and Sikhism. This kind of love is not biased, i.e., not restricted toward only dear ones. It is extended towards all living beings. As Buddhist maintained this type of love (*Metta*) enables one to regard all as fellow-beings. Or as taught in Sikhism, this love is without any selection or exclusion. I will explain this form of love a bit further while explaining the relevant section.

Overview

Overall, this chapter details the following points about compassion:

- Compassion, as the etymology of this word suggests, is the *feeling* felt *with the* sufferer.[70]
- Although the feeling of compassion like pity and sympathy is evoked by the perception of the other's negative condition, yet they are not synonymous terms. Pity, unlike compassion includes a stance of superiority towards its object that is expressed in condescension. And moreover, it lacks the active concern for the sufferers' well-being. Sympathy, like pity, is not a synonym of compassion, as it also lacks the desire to relieve the sufferer. But feeling of sympathy can be understood as a part of compassion, as both includes fellow-feeling with the sufferer.
- Different philosophers assumed different types of relationship between compassion-feeler and compassionate-object. Some believe that this relationship is formed by imagination; some believe it is a result of recognition of our-own vulnerability; while others maintain that it is based on love. I summarize below:

- Three kinds of imaginations have been mentioned above and only the third one (i.e., a strong and powerful imagination) is satisfactory in making the relationship between the compassionate subject and the sufferer.
- But Aristotle and Snow maintain that the *recognition of our own vulnerability* is a necessary requirement to make compassion possible. Here, at the heart of this link is the belief that "*it could be me*".
- There are two parameters on which love is defined. The first is more prevalent in the contemporary world, and the second in religious philosophy and practices.

A discussion of all these assumed relationships by different philosophers creates ambiguity in one's mind about the nature of compassion and how it arises between the subject and the sufferer. I raised this matter and other relevant issues earlier in the introduction. I would further analyze this relationship in the adjoining chapters.

2

Nature of Compassion; Aristotle, Aquinas and Nussbaum

This chapter will discuss Western views of compassion through centuries. I start with Aristotle's view of compassion, and then I move on to Aquinas' view. In the next section I proceed to analyze Nussbaum's views and some of its criticisms. Besides the impartial exposition of the notion of compassion by these philosophers, this chapter will also analyze the set of questions raised in the introduction.

Before proceeding further I think it is important to note that *compassion* is a contemporary term and cannot be traced back to any specific era of early Western philosophy. But this does not mean that there was no sense of compassion in the early Western world. Compassion has existed ever since the man found himself to be social. It was also present in the early Western world, but the gesture was expressed through different names. 'It is believed that Greek's tragic terms *eleos* and *oiktos* had the same connotation as compassion has. After some time, Greek *eleos* and *oiktos* got rendered into classical Latin by *Misericordia*, and both of these into Italian by *pieta*, into French by *pitie*. All of these, in turn, are translated into English by pity – although the British moral philosophers of eighteenth century sometimes used the term 'sympathy'. In German, meanwhile, *Mitleid* is the word most commonly chosen to translate the Greek, Latin, and French words, although *Mitgefuhl* also occurs. English can at times render *Mitlied* (literally) by compassion.'[71] I've constructed the following chart for a better and easier understanding:

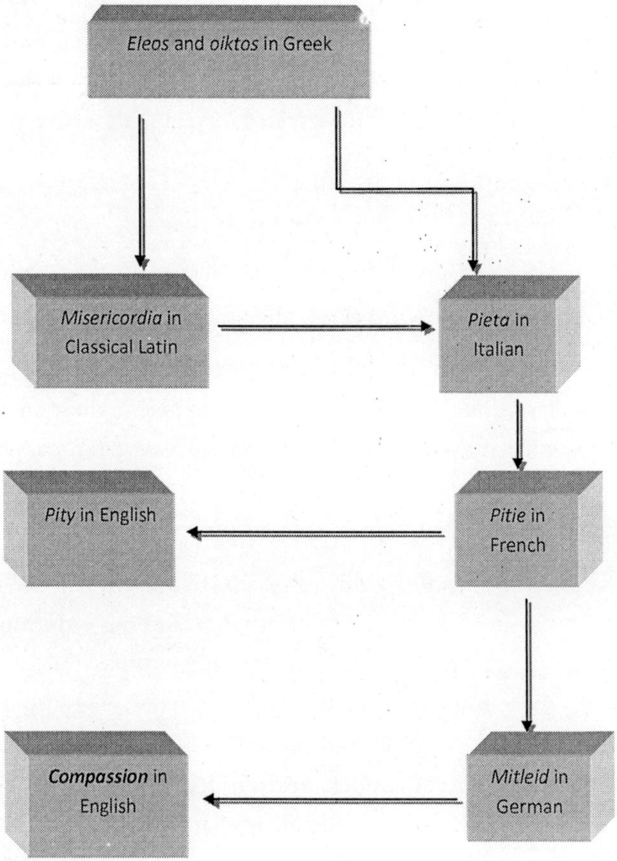

Aristotle's Notion of Compassion

Aristotle discussed the feeling of compassion at some length in book II of the *Rhetorica*. The term *Eleos*[72] is used by him to define this feeling. He defined it 'as a feeling of pain caused by the sight of some evil, destructive or painful, which befalls one who does not deserve it, and which we might expect to befall ourselves or some friends of ours, and moreover to us soon.'[73] For him, it is not only a feeling but an emotion,[74] and like other major emotions it has an intimate relation with cognition. It is Aristotle's view that to arouse every emotion the knowledge of following three constituents are necessary.

1. The things that excite our emotions,[75]
2. The people on whom we bestow emotions[76], and
3. The subject's (who feels) the state of mind.[77]

According to Aristotle, all these points are necessary to arouse any kind of emotion. We would not be able to arouse these emotions even if any one of these is lacking.[78] In the case of compassion all these points can be understood simply by analyzing the very definition of compassion as stated above. Let's analyze them one by one.

First is the ground or things that excite our emotions. In the case of compassion, the suffering of other excites our emotion. For Aristotle only serious sufferings excite our compassion, and he categorizes these serious sufferings into two types: '[1] unpleasant and painful things[79] and [2] evil caused by luck.'[80] Representative examples of the former includes: death in its various forms, bodily injuries and afflictions, old age, diseases, lack of food[81]. Examples of the latter includes: friendlessness, scarcity of friends (it is a pitiful thing to be torn away from friends and companions), deformity, weakness, mutilation; evil coming from a source from which good ought to have come; and the frequent repetition of such misfortunes[82]. Also the coming of good when the worst has happened: e.g., a poor person winning a lottery, but getting the money after death[83]. Included are examples where either no good should have befallen a man at all, or that he should not be able to enjoy it when it has.[84]

Second, compassion is felt for persons who do not deserve suffering. Aristotle maintains that where we judge that the suffering is brought on by the agent's own bad choices, we do not feel compassionate for him. We move only for those cases where we believe that the agent is of noble character and the misfortune on an agent comes not because of his mistakes. In this way, in order to feel compassion, one must believe in the goodness of other; if one thinks that nobody is good, then it means he or she believes that everybody deserves evil fortune.[85]

Third, the one who feels compassion also feels pain, because he believes that the sufferer is like him and does not deserve suffering. Moreover, to feel compassion a person must be capable of remembering that similar misfortune had happened to me or my friends, or expecting them to happen in future. In this manner it is closely connected with the belief that I myself can be vulnerable in similar ways, as others are. Aristotle maintained when the sufferings of others are close to us then they excite our compassion.[86] For example, we are compassionate about those who are like us – in age, character, disposition, social standing, or birth; for in all these cases we can see similarities with other people, and thus it appears more likely that the same misfortune may befall us also.[87] He further maintained we do not feel compassion for those cases where there is a lack of connection.[88] For example, 'we cannot remember what disasters happened a hundred centuries ago, nor do we look forward to what will happen a hundred centuries hereafter, and therefore feel little pity [compassion], if any.'[89] He suggests that we feel compassion for only those people who are related to us, since in these cases we feel about them as if we ourselves were in danger.[90] This happens because we have acknowledgement that we feel fear when the danger is near us.[91] In short, one's ability to identify with others is promoted by his belief that he is similar to them. When one feels compassion for others, that is, when he identifies with others in their plight, he recognizes various similarities between himself and others. The recognition of this vulnerability, both his own and that of others, act as a bond that can enable the person who feels compassion. At the heart of this link is the belief that we are similar to those in distress to be able to experience misfortune also. This belief can be expressed in the thought "that it could be me."

Aristotle Categorizes Number of Classes of People Who Have these Supposed Capabilities

1. Those who think evil may befall on them, such as those who have already had it befallen on them and have safely escaped from it;[92]
   a. Elderly men, owing to their good sense and experience.[93]
   b. Weak men, especially men inclined to cowardice.[94]
   c. And also educated people, since they have a larger perspective of evil.[95]
2. Also those who have parents living, or children, or wives; for these are our own, and the evils mentioned above may easily befall them.[96]

According to Aristotle, there are two kinds of people who do not feel compassion for the sufferings of others. First, compassion is not aroused by those who believe that he or she is so badly off that nothing bad could further happen to them to make things worse.[97] The second are those people who believe they have very good fortune, thus bad could not happen to them.[98] The former ones generally believe that they are completely ruined, and also suppose that no further evil can befall them.[99] They are not able to feel compassion for the sufferer because they look at the sufferer's plight from the very bottom, from the point of view of one whose sufferings are complete. For example, suppose a very poor man who met with a serious accident and is going to die in few hours, as he has no money for treatment. He is badly suffering as his whole body is bleeding. Now, when this man sees some other suffering person, he might feel no compassion for him, as he might see other's plight from the point of view of one whose suffering is complete.[100] On the other hand, the latter (second kind of people- who do not feel compassionate) believe that they are self-sufficient, secure in their possession of the good life.[101] They normally suppose that what happens to others cannot possibly happen to themselves. For example, suppose there's a billionaire who had never faced any kind of suffering nor has any fear of the future. Such a person, I think, according to Aristotle, would not be able to feel compassion.

He further maintained that the emotion of compassion can be felt only by those who are between two extremes, i.e., courageous emotion (such as anger or confidence) and great fear or insolence.[102] Because those who are moved by courageous emotions such as anger or confidence take 'no account of the possibility that something evil can happen to them, and even an insolent man and panic stricken people do not take account of the future.'[103] That's why only those men who are between these two extremes can feel compassion.

From the Above Account I Come to the following Analysis

Compassion for Aristotle is a painful emotion, which is based on both external cognitive elements (e.g., the external suffering) and internal cognitive elements (i.e., the sufferer does not deserve suffering, and the mental belief that 'it could be me').

Aristotle defined compassion as a painful emotion; it means that this emotion involves sorrow or suffering on the part of those who feels this emotion. But he did not clearly explain the nature of this suffering. Even in the above account, it is quite observable that this suffering is caused either by past bad memories or fear for the future, yet it is not very clear whether the subject suffers with the same intensity as the sufferer is suffering or not. I think from the above discussion it follows that the compassionate-subject suffers some kind of psychological pain, but the intensity of this pain is not the same as the sufferer. If, like Aristotle, we assume that the compassionate-subject's suffering is because of his own past memories, then it might be possible that the subject feels either far more or less pain from the sufferer, as he is not relating with the actual suffering but only with his own personal experiences. Further, if the compassionate subject is suffering out of the fear of the same evil happening to him (as explained earlier), then also it is not a surety that he will suffer with the same intensity as the sufferer, as it is possible he could well blow the actual situation out of proportion under a phobia.

For Aristotle, compassion is a response towards only those sufferings which causes serious pain. He gave a list of serious sufferings, which might seem little to us, but we should remember that the complexities and tragedies of modern life did not exist in his time. He further maintained that we do not feel compassion for ignoble person or for those people who have brought suffering on themselves. This assertion seems a little problematic to me. It is right that in some cases we do not feel compassion for those who cause suffering for themselves. For example, it is quite difficult for a normal human being to feel compassion for a rapist who is punished. But in many cases we do feel compassion for a person who has earned suffering for himself because of his free choices.

For example, many people definitely feel compassion on an injured person who enters into the fire to save a child. Here one can point out, as Aristotle also maintained that, we feel compassion for a person who has noble character. But I think here we feel compassion not because X has a noble character, but because he got injured by doing noble deeds, as it is not necessary that a noble charactered person always perform nobly.[104]

For Aristotle, the *capability of remembrance or the supposition* plays a role in the relationship between the compassion-feeler and the compassionate-object. This assumption, I think, and as Carr[105] also believes, makes Aristotle's account a self-centered one, as one feels compassion for another either because his past restricted bad memories or because of his fears. That is, one becomes capable of identifying with the victims' distress because one believes that he too or those close to him can face the same misfortune as the victim is facing. Here 'fear' plays a key role in achieving an understanding of, and feeling for, suffering people. Thus, in this account, the subject feels compassion out of fear and not because of genuine concerns.

Until now I have analyzed the nature of compassion in Aristotle's account. I will now take up the further analysis of compassion in Aquinas' account.

Aquinas on Compassion

In *Summa Theologiæ*, St. Thomas Aquinas sets himself to find the nature of compassion under the heading of *misericórdia. Misericórdia* is a Latin word, which literally means "having a miserable heart". Aquinas also maintained that *misericórdia* gets its name from denoting a person's compassionate heart (***miseum cor***) for1 another's unhappiness.[106]

The concept of "another's unhappiness" or "misery" is important to his discussion. Unhappy is he who does not have what he desires. In Aquinas words, unhappiness and misery implies that a man suffers against his will.[107] He observes that there are three kinds of miseries in this life. First, there is the suffering that goes against our natural appetite for existence and life, such as the misery of a sick man.[108] Secondly, there is suffering that strikes us suddenly and unexpectedly, such as sufferings arising from accidents.[109] The third kind of suffering strikes a person when he consistently pursues the good, yet he meets only overpowering evil.[110] St. Thomas here has in mind Aristotle's remark that 'mercy is especially called for when misfortune afflicts a man who has not deserved it.'[111]

According to Aquinas, compassion is "heartfelt sympathy for another's distress, impelling us to succor him if we can."[112] He discusses compassion as an interior effect of charity, a theological virtue.[113] It is interior because compassion is felt within the person who has charity.[114] The cause of it, charity, Aquinas describes as the friendship between God's children and God Himself.

Aquinas argues that the human virtue of mercy necessarily should be both affective and effective. Affective mercy is an emotion: the sympathy we feel for the plight of another.[115] Effective mercy, on the other hand, is something that we do, a positive action for the good of another, taking steps to relieve the miseries or meet the needs of others.[116] Aquinas believes that if we merely "sympathize" with the plight of another and "share their pain" without making the best of the opportunities we have to help them, then the virtue of mercy does not abide in us in any significant degree.[117] Thus mercy is a feeling for the others' misery, accompanied with an action to help. But here the question arises as to how one can feel the suffering of others. According to Aquinas, this happens in two ways;

first, one looks upon another's misery as one's own, through being united to him by love, and second, on account of the possibility of suffering in the same way.[118]

Describing the first, Aquinas says, "He who loves another looks upon his friend as another self, he counts his friend's hurt as his own, so that he grieves for his friend's hurt as though he were hurt himself. As Aristotle reckons grieving with one's friend as being one of the signs of friendship, and the Apostle says (Rom. Xii. 15): rejoice with them that rejoice, weep with them that weep."[119]

Secondly, human mercy is grounded in a "defect" in our nature: the defect of human vulnerability to suffering. We feel pity for those who suffer because we too are subjected to such miseries.[120] Aquinas notes Aristotle's saying that 'men pity such as are akin to them, and the like, because it makes them realize that the same may happen to themselves. This also explains why old and the wise who consider that they may fall upon evil times, as also feeble and timorous persons, are more inclined to pity: whereas those who deem themselves happy, and so far powerful as to think themselves in no danger of suffering any hurt, are no[t] so inclined to pity.'[121]

Aquinas also insists that compassion should be extended to our enemies.[122] In his discussion of charity, he suggests that we should love our enemies in a general sense, in accord with their nature. After all they too are our neighbors.[123]

Aquinas describes compassion as a virtue. According to him, compassion is not simply an ephemeral feeling. It comes from the will, the rational desire. As he writes, 'this movement is regulated by reason.'[124] In other words, it involves choice, since we choose to extend compassion to someone. He further suggests that compassion is among the greatest of virtues, as he writes, "Of all the virtues which relate to our neighbor, mercy is the greatest."[125]

From the Above, the Following Analysis of Compassion Can be Made

Aquinas defines compassion as a fellow-feeling (heartfelt-sympathy)[126] for another's plight, which is either caused by love or by recognition of our-own vulnerability. He defined it as fellow-feeling, means sharing the very feeling of another. It further means that compassion by its very definition involves pain or sorrow. But what kind of pain is involved is not clear. I think we can find the answer by analyzing the very concept of compassion as defined by him. As we already know, he recognizes love as an important link that makes a relationship between compassionate-subject and sufferer, since when one loves somebody, he automatically gets attached with that person, and due to this attachment, feels other's pain and sorrow as his own. Thus, here, the intensity of the pain and sorrow can be understood by analyzing the concept of love. In love we feel the pain of others due to an attachment. And as we know attachments are not only biased but also vary due to our own mental projections. And we may imagine more pain than there actually is. Thus, in this way, due to the attachment, the intensity of the pain felt can be significantly higher than what the sufferer himself feels.

Further, for Aquinas there are two ways by which relationship between the compassion-feeler and the sufferer can be made. As we have already seen in love the relation is made due to the attachment. For Aquinas love not only means to have affectionate attachment with only the dear ones, but according to him, we should extend our love to our enemies also- who are not our dear ones. The second element that is 'recognition of our-own vulnerability' causes a relationship between compassionate-subject and sufferer is same as the Aristotelian element of 'capability of supposing', i.e., we too are vulnerable as others are.

Despite the fact that Aquinas' account also rests on the element of *fear*, this account seems quite altruistic in nature. He defined it as a virtue which involves a rational desire of help. Here the compassionate-person feels for another not only because of the possibility of his own vulnerability, but also because of the genuine concern for other's well-being. Moreover, this account of compassion is accompanied with the action of help for the sufferer in best possible cases.

Now let us move to the notion of compassion as defined by Nussbaum:

Nussbaum's Account of Compassion

Nussbaum develops her account of compassion explicitly on the basis of Aristotle's account of compassion. But, while adopting Aristotle's account Nussbaum did not directly import it into her account of compassion; she made some significant changes in it. Like Aristotle, Nussbaum too believes that compassion is an emotion. She maintains that compassion is a complex evaluative judgment made up of three cognitive components: first, judgment of size; second, the judgment of non desert and the third is eudemonistic judgment. She keeps Aristotle's first and second cognitive requirements, but replaces his third requirement with that of similar possibilities with an explicitly eudemonistic requirement.

Thus, Nussbaum's account offers an addition on Aristotle's account. That's why while adopting the first cognitive requirement of Aristotle's account, she didn't forget to put her own contribution in it. Like Aristotle, she too believes that compassion involves the recognition that a serious bad event has befallen on someone. But, unlike him, she didn't construct a limited list of serious plights. She maintains that societies (and individuals) vary to some degree in what they take to be a serious plight; they vary, too, in the level of damage required before something is taken to be a serious plight.[127] She called this requirement a 'judgment of size.'[128]

Here she also makes clear that compassion is a judgment based on an observer's point of view. She gives three examples to explain the same:

> The first example is the *loss of reason*. Suppose a person has altogether lost the use of reason. This man, for Nussbaum, is an object of compassion to anyone who has 'the least spark of humanity.'[129]

The second example is of *peacocks' tongues*. Q, a Roman aristocrat, discovers that his shipment of peacocks' tongues from Africa has been interrupted. Feeling that his dinner party that evening will be a total disaster in consequence, he weeps in bitter tears, and implores his friend Seneca to pity him. Seneca laughs.[130]

The third example is that of *uneducated rural woman*. A woman (R) in rural India, severely under-nourished and poorly educated, has no idea what it is to feel healthy and has no idea of the benefits and pleasures of education. So thoroughly has she internalized her culture's views of what is right for women, that she believes that she is living a good and flourishing life. The workers in the province's rural development agency feel deeply moved and think that something must be done.[131]

From these examples Nussbaum resolves that the onlooker judges the seriousness of the other's suffering. Or compassion takes up the onlooker's point of view. Here, 'onlooker's judgment' means the judgment made by the subject.[132] This judgment can be different from his (subject's) personal judgment; for the subject may judge that the sufferer is right to accord importance to a certain sort of loss, even though he himself does not do so.[133] We can understand this with the help of the following example given by Nussbaum, of a wind player whose lip is slightly injured. In normal circumstances, I might have compassion on his condition, because I will judge his suffering to be of tremendous size, as I can see it is a terrible thing to be deprived of one's career and one's mode of expression. But on this same account I would not expect compassion on myself from others since the injury that would mean loss of career to him means no such thing to me. And this general description also validates the judgment of "size."[134]

Nussbaum, like Aristotle, also believes that the subject will blame and reproach him, rather than having compassion, if he finds that the sufferer has created misfortune for himself.

Insofar as we do feel compassion, it is either because we believe the person to be without blame for her plight or because, though there is an element of fault, we believe that her suffering is out of proportion to the fault. Compassion then addresses itself to the non-blameworthy increment.[135]

Nussbaum further maintains that compassion requires blamelessness not only on the part of its object, but also on the part of the onlooker. Because it would be simply hypocritical, for a subject, to weep over a plight that he himself has caused.

> *.........the onlooker has to see the disaster as falling on the person from outside, so to speak; and she will be unable to do this if she believes either that the person has caused it or that she herself has caused it.*[136]

Here, Nussbaum also points out that people sometimes have compassion for those whose plights are, in large part, their own creation. For example, a parent may feel compassion on the plight of their adolescent child, who has come to grief through his own fault. Nussbaum believes that such kind of thoughts brings a two-stage judgment; first, it is the child's own fault and second, we think that the condition of adolescence is not his fault as it brings with it certain obliviousness and a liability to certain kinds of misplays. She further holds that we seem to feel compassion only on those errors which are a part of the predicament of adolescence and not on all kinds of blunders. For example, we can easily feel compassionate for a teenager who has been arrested for drunk driving, but not for one who has tortured and killed a dog[137]. The latter does not seem to be a part of any kind of "bad fate" - his actions do not leave any space for any sort of consideration - 'not even the consideration of the "bad fate" of being sixteen.'[138]

Thus, according to Nussbaum, compassion requires the belief that there are serious bad things that may happen to people through no fault of their own. It means that in order to have compassion for another, the compassionate person accepts a certain picture of the world, a picture according to which the valuable things are not always safely under a person's own control, but liable to damage by fortune. But how valuable are these things? From whose point of view are these things valuable, or which things should get the status of valuable things, is yet another set of issues.[139]

Now, as far as the third requirement of compassion is concerned, Nussbaum's account departs from Aristotle's account. Aristotle insists that compassion requires acknowledgment that one has possibilities and vulnerabilities similar to those of the sufferer. One makes sense of the suffering by recognizing that one might oneself or someone close to him may encounter such plights. Here, compassion is closely linked to fear. But, in Nussbaum's account, the requirement of similar possibilities is unnecessary, as it makes the definition of compassion too restrictive. To make it clear, she points out the cases of compassion felt by superior beings (like God or gods) for the misfortunes of inferior ones (mortal beings), despite the fact that divine beings are not vulnerable to the same misfortunes as we mortals are.

> *..........the gods are depicted as obtuse and lacking in compassion; this lack is connected to their lack of vulnerability. .... but gods (and godlike humans) sometimes do have compassion. Zeus weeps for the death of sarpedon; the Christian god feels ceaseless compassion for the errors and suffering of mortals; the Buddhist who has successfully escaped from the personal vulnerability and pain experiences compassion for the sufferings of those still fettered. .... The Christian god is vulnerable in a similar way, suffering agony and death both in his own person and in the person of his son. The bodhisattva has experienced the ills that he pities, even if by now he no longer expects to do so.*[140]

Here, she is trying to exert that God wouldn't feel compassion for our misfortune if he sees us as strange or puny to be worth the bother. For this reason, Nussbaum didn't drop Aristotle's requirement of similar possibilities. Rather she replaces it with an explicitly eudaimonistic requirement; a requirement that one sees the well-being of the object of one's compassion as important and takes it as one's end.[141] She observes that the judgment of similar possibility is part of a construct that bridges the gap between the child's existing goals and the eudaimonistic judgment that others are an important part of one's own scheme of goals and projects, important as ends in their own right. Now, it is important to know how this eudaimonistic judgment is formed by person. According to Nussbaum, 'Equipped with her general conception of human flourishing, the spectator looks at a world in which people suffer hunger, disability, disease, slavery, through no fault of their own.'[142] And she believes that goods such as food, health, citizenship, freedom do matter.[143] Although she is one amongst the safe and privileged whom such goods are stably guaranteed,[144] yet she acknowledges that she cannot overlook the possibility of her being in a misfortunate condition, - that beggary might come his way. 'This leads her to turn her thoughts outwards, asking society's general arrangement for the allocation of goods and resources.'[145] By realizing the uncertainty of life, she inclines to the want of a society in which the lot of the worst off -of the poor, of people defeated in war, of women, of servants- is as good as it can be.[146]

From this, it follows that the recognition of one's own related vulnerability is, then, an important and frequently an indispensable epistemological requirement for compassion in human beings – the thing that makes the difference between viewing hungry peasants as beings whose sufferings matter and viewing them as distant objects whose experiences have nothing to do with one's own life. Such an imagination is psychologically powerful in moving other people into one's own circle of concern. For example, when we feel compassion for animals, which are very different from ourselves, it is only on the basis of our common vulnerability to pain, hunger, and other types of suffering that we feel the emotion. Even when we talk about their lack of legal rights, their lack of power to shape the laws that affect their lives, or (in some cases) their lack of understanding of what is happening to them – it is most often on the basis of a sense of shared vulnerability to pain that we extend our compassion. Here, we imagine that how horrible it would be to suffer pain in that way. Judging that one is similarly vulnerable to the misfortunes that have befallen another is, Nussbaum suggests, a valuable way of coming to realize the importance of another's well-being and to take it as one's end, but it is this realization and not the judgment of similar possibilities that is strictly necessary to compassion[147]. In other words, the eudaimonistic judgment, not the judgment of similar possibilities is a necessary constituent of compassion. As we have seen above, a truly loving deity can be concerned for human suffering without thinking of its own risks. Thus, Nussbaum claims that, in order for compassion to be present, the person must consider the suffering of another as a significant part of his or her own scheme of goals and ends. However, imagining one's own similar possibilities aids the extension of one's own eudaimonistic imagination.

A Further Conceptual Consideration of Nussbaum's Account by Brain Carr

As I have already discussed, Nussbaum's develops her account of compassion on the basis of Aristotle's account. She extends it making some significant changes such that Brain Carr writes, 'the way in which Nussbaum develops her account is much more promising than that of Aristotle's Rhetoric'.[148] She holds, as stated above, that compassion has three cognitive elements: the first is judgment of size (a serious bad event has befallen someone); second is the judgment of non-desertion (this person did not bring the suffering on himself or herself); and the third is *eudemonistic judgment* (this person, or creature, is a significant element in my scheme of goals and projects, an end whose good is to be promoted).[149] But for Carr, Aristotle's and subsequently Nussbaum's account seems to render compassion as a self-centered emotion. Aristotle's account rests on the idea of similar possibilities. As Carr points out, what arouses compassion, on Aristotle's account, is determined by what we are, and this is one clear respect in which his account is quite self-centered.[150] In this way, on his account, we do not feel compassion for people in Idi Amin's Uganda.[151] Another feature that renders Aristotle's account of pity a self-centered emotion is that he omits any account of the volitional dimension of pity. Here, volitional dimension means 'some reference to the subject being moved to help the one who is suffering.'[152] And, without the volitional dimension, the account has overlooked a part of altruism which marks off pity and compassion from other emotions such as envy, hatred, appetite and fear.[153] Nussbaum's account of compassion is an improvement over Aristotle's account. Unlike Aristotle's account, Nussbaum's account, as we have discussed above, rests on the eudaimonistic judgment. But for Carr, Nussbaum's account is a self-centered one, because her accounts also fail to show altruistic concern.

According to Carr, compassion is an altruistic emotion, which consists of three features, namely cognitive, affective and volition. That is: (1.) it involves an appreciation of the suffering under which another labours; (2.) it involves a sympathetic reaction of distress on the part of the agent- the one who feels compassion; (3.) it involves the agent's being moved if possible to help to alleviate that suffering.[154] According to him, in Nussbaum's account the volitional feature of compassion is missing, which make her account a self-centered one. Compassion, for Carr takes us out of ourselves into the hearts and minds of other people, and makes compassion function thereby as an important social virtue.

Further he identifies a problem in Nussbaum's account with the assertion that 'compassion takes up the onlooker's point of view'. She gives three examples (loss of reason, peacocks' tongues, and uneducated rural women)[155] to prove her point. But, Carr points out that her very readiness to defend her beliefs clearly manifests her failure to capture the altruism of compassion.[156] He believes that it is right to say that the sight of serious suffering generates a compassionate feeling in the person. But only from these three examples it would be too quick to conclude that the onlooker is the judge of seriousness of suffering in all cases.[157] For Carr, Nussbaum's criterion of 'assessment of size' is problematic, as she is imposing her own value judgment on the sufferer. Carr maintains that compassion, by its very definition, involves a shared experience of suffering, even though the degrees and kinds of suffering could well be very different in the one who feels compassion, and in one for whom compassion is felt.[158] According to him, 'those who suffer but do not feel their suffering might well be candidates for pity, but could not be the candidates for compassion.'[159] Here one thing is important to note, that Carr makes a distinction between felt and unfelt suffering. The 'felt suffering' is suffering which is actually experienced by the sufferer, while 'unfelt suffering' is not experienced by the sufferer[160]. Examples of unfelt suffering include, as earlier mentioned, a financial loss in which 'I' suffer, but which I am unaware of; or the death of a distant relative which never comes to my attention; or a permanent comatose state which I suffer after an accident.[161] With the help of this distinction, Carr points out that compassion is based on felt suffering and not on the unfelt suffering, because, as the etymology of the word suggests it is 'suffering with the sufferer.'[162] Nussbaum's first and third example 'the loss of reason case and the uneducated rural women' cases are both examples of the unfelt suffering. In these cases, the people in bad conditions are unable to feel suffering, or we can say they are not in a state to comprehend their own condition. Here, the onlooker cannot feel with the sufferer, because of the very nature of suffering. And in the case of peacock tongue, Carr's reaction is quite different from Nussbaum's. He asserts that the obvious problem with the case of Q's suffering is that we might find his value system so alienated that we might well reject his suffering and do not feel related to it.[163] But compassion, as suggested by him, is not a rejection of those values which are alien to us, since it involves a consideration of other people's values, beliefs, needs and wants in terms of which their suffering can be understood and hence be shared[164].

According to Carr, Nussbaum's rejection, along with Seneca, of Q's system of values may well be what blocks her compassion.[165] He further maintains that it would be too quick to take the example as supporting the general claim that the onlooker is the judge of seriousness of the suffering in all cases.[166] And it would imply that only such suffering as is premised on the values and beliefs of the onlooker could be taken seriously as cause for a sympathetic response. In other words, it means one would always be imposing his own values and beliefs on others, or simply turning away from them as morally reprehensible or fools.[167] And, we know this is not compassion. On the contrary, compassion involves our moving out of ourselves into the misfortunes of others who are not necessarily like us.

Here, while criticizing Nussbaum I think Carr is drifting slightly in the wrong direction, since Nussbaum also believes that compassion is not imposing our own values on victim, but it involves moving out of ourselves into the victim's misfortune, as she exemplifies this in her 'wind-players' example.[168] Here I should elucidate that I am not supporting Nussbaum for adding a clause of *judgment*, i.e., compassion-feeler (onlooker) judges the seriousness of suffering, as I also feel that this clause is quite problematic. I would critically analyze this issue further while concluding this dissertation.

Further Carr criticizes Nussbaum on adding a clause of blamelessness in the definition of compassion. Nussbaum suggests that 'insofar as we believe that a person came to grief through his or her own fault, we will blame and reproach him', and not feel compassionate towards him.[169] Carr gives an example refuting Nussbaum's approach.

Suppose a professional solider............ [who] in his enthusiasm for the honour of the regiment and his own promotion, just suffered horrific injuries and is carried off to the field hospital. Would we blame and reproach? Would we dismiss him from our minds for his foolish profession and its likely outcome? I think we would rather respond with greater sympathy, and feel compassion for his suffering. The fault was his own, but the 'least spark of humanity' demands an appreciation of very real suffering which that fault has produced. And what of the relatives- parents, siblings, wife- who have tolerated or indeed encouraged this foolhardy profession, but must now live with its consequences? The fault was theirs, but their suffering calls up our compassion nevertheless. We cannot just turn away and reject them as fools. If we did so we would be once more imposing our value system upon them.[170]

Here Carr is trying to point out that perhaps it is not so difficult to understand the soldier's action in terms of family tradition, the desire for regimental and personal honour, the wish to push one self to the limit and prove oneself against undeniable dangers, indeed the desire for financial gain for one's skills and one's risks.[171] He further maintained that certainly we might not choose such a profession.[172] But to reserve our compassion, by seeing the suffering as due to the sufferer's own culpable actions would be hardhearted and manifest an intolerance of others' choices and ways of life. Thus, one cannot reserve his compassion by such clauses, since compassion means to transcend our own personal judgments and understand the situation in terms of the sufferer's heart and mind.

From the above discussion it follows that Carr rightly points out the flaws of Nussbaum's account. I agree with most of Carr's views for the following reasons:

- I think Carr is right in holding the view that compassion without the action of help (without its volition feature, as he defined) will lose its altruistic nature. To understand it better take an example of a man who feels bad for an old lady unable to cross the road, but not ready to move a bit for help. Although it is right that in many case an action of help is not possible, but one should help at least in those cases where it is possible. I would illustrate this point further in later discussion.

- Second, I also agree that compassion can only be felt in 'felt case'. For instance y believes that the person x is unhappy while actually x feels that he is happy, then it is only y's observation, his personal feeling, and not x's suffering that causes compassion. Here one might object by portraying an example of an infant who is facing some stomach ache, but is not able to comprehend his problem. In this case, would not most of us feel compassion for this infant since he is not in a position to comprehend his own suffering? To this I would rather answer 'yes', it is right that by seeing the suffering of an infant we would be compassionate towards him. Here one thing is important to remember that the infant is not able to comprehend the cause of pain, but is very much able to feel the pain. So in this case we are *feeling with the sufferer* and not only *feeling for the sufferer.* While in 'R-case' of Nussbaum the sufferer is neither able to comprehend her pain nor able to feel it.
- I also agree with Carr that compassion does not always include the clause of blamelessness, as many times we are compassionate for the sufferer either because he is regretting his deed or because his action is for some noble deed or simply because we are not aware of his full condition. And, moreover sometimes only because of love and attachment. I would illustrate these points in my later chapters and in the conclusion.

Now let's move to the next important question which has been little discussed in the previous sections, i.e., whether compassion is an emotion or a virtue?

Is Compassion an Emotion or a Virtue?

It is a matter of debate as to whether compassion is an emotion or a virtue. According to Aristotle[173] and Nussbaum[174] it is an emotion. But some philosophers like Brian Carr,[175] St. Aquinas,[176] and Gregory E. Pence,[177] believe that it (compassion) is a virtue. It is important here to know the difference between virtue and emotion.

We can understand 'virtue' and 'emotion' within the Aristotelian line of thought. According to him, virtues are a 'state of character' and emotions are feelings distinct from bodily sensations, as they involve cognition. He claimed that there are two types of emotions: first, practical; and second, non-practical.[178] Practical emotions are those which involve a particular kind of goal and normally manifest themselves in particular goal directed behavior.[179] For example, anger is a practical emotion aiming at revenge.[180] On the opposite, non-practical emotion does not involve any goal nor manifest them in any goal directed behavior. Compassion is an example of non-practical emotion, as feeling compassion is, for Aristotle, compatible with doing nothing.[181] And only 'practice emotions' invite virtue in the sense of practical disposition to choose an act.

In *Nicomachean Ethics,* Aristotle cited the following differences between emotion and virtue:[182] First, a man is neither blamed nor praised for the particular emotion he feels, but he is praised or blamed for his virtue and vices.[183] Second, virtues, unlike emotions, involve choices or are modes of choice.[184] Third, in respect to emotion, persons are said to be moved, i.e., persons feel emotions, like fear, anger, without choice.[185] But, on the other hand, virtues are not simply to be moved, they involve choices. The virtue lies in the way in which an emotion is felt and not in the simple feeling of the emotion as such. Thus, virtues are the disposition of characters. Fifth, virtues fall at a mean between two extreme character traits, i.e., between excess and deficiency:

> *...it is this [moral virtue] that is concerned with emotions and actions, and in these there is excess, defect, and the intermediate. For instance, both fear and confidence and appetite and anger and pity and in general pleasure and pain may be felt both too much and too little, and in both cases not well; but to feel them at the right times, with reference to the right objects, towards the right people, with the right motive, and in the right way, is what is both intermediate and best, and this characteristic of virtue.*[186]

From these Distinctions the Following Observations can be Made

- As we have already discussed above, according to Aristotle, compassion is an emotion. It is quite clear that for him compassion is a non-practical emotion, as it does not manifest itself into goal directed behavior. In simple words, any aim or goal (e.g., any action of help) is not attached with this feeling. But it is a puzzle that if it is only an emotion then why, in *Rhetoric*, has he defined it as a means between two excesses, courageous emotion (such as anger or confidence) and great fear.
- As far as Aquinas's notion of compassion is concerned, there is no confusion in it: He clearly states that it is a virtue which involves reason.[187]
- Nussbaum proclaimed compassion as an emotion. But the characteristics she attached with this feeling are like a virtue. She maintained that reason and choices are involved in the act of compassion.[188] And above we have seen that virtue involves choices and reason.

Overview

This chapter reveals the nature of compassion by looking at how different philosophers in the West describe it. This chapter also contends that although there is no one uniform definition of the term, there is yet one little and linear thread, on which the philosophers move around. As we have seen above, Aquinas's and Nussbaum's accounts are not only an extension of the Aristotelian account of compassion, but are definitely a step forward. However, sharing a common thought that compassion arises by the sight of suffering, all these philosophers tend to disagree on many points.

Firstly, they do not agree that compassion is an emotion. For Aristotle and Nussbaum, it is an emotion, while for Aquinas and Carr, it is a virtue. From the above discussion it is clear that compassion involves the characteristics of virtue as it involves choice factor and reason, and it is a mean between the two excess.

Second, according to the Aristotelian and Aquinas's account, compassion involves pain and sorrow. Although it is not clear with what intensity a compassionate-subject suffers, it is clear that it can't be same as that of the sufferer. That is compassionate-subject either feels more suffering or less suffering than the sufferer. On the other hand, I think, Nussbaum gets by this question well, i.e., whether compassion involves suffering or not, as she defines compassion as an evaluative judgment.

Third, according to Aristotle's and Nussbaum's account, compassion does not include the action of help. While, for Aquinas compassion includes the action of help in best possible cases.

Fourth, all these philosophers have different views on the question on how the relationship between compassion-feeler and compassionate-subject is formed. From the above accounts, four types of relationship are followed: the first type of relationship is formed by 'capability of remembrance or supposition' (as maintained by Aristotle); the second type of relationship is formed by 'love' (Aquinas); the third type of relationship is formed by 'eudaimonistic judgment' (Nussbaum); and the fourth one by 'imagination' (Carr). I will critically analyze all these relationships in the final conclusion of my dissertation.

3

Nature of Compassion: Buddhism and Sikhism

This chapter presents the views of *Theravāda* Buddhism and Sikhism on the nature of compassion. I start with the exposition and analysis of *Theravāda* Buddhists' account. In the subsequent section, I proceed with the discussion of compassion according to Sikhism. In both the sections, an attempt has been made to resolve the set of questions raised in the introduction around which the study of the nature of compassion revolves. I then move on to analyze the cases that were mentioned in the previous chapter (raised originally by Nussbaum) with reference to both Buddhism and Sikhism.

Buddhists' Account of Compassion

Compassion is central to Buddhist teachings. The concept of compassion is emphasized in both earlier and later Buddhist teachings. Here, I will be discussing compassion on the basis of selected Theravāda Buddhist texts (primarily Buddhaghoṣa's *Visuddhimagga*[189] with some references to *Pāḷi* Canon texts such as ***Dhammapada***). The *Theravāda* school is one of the early schools of Buddhism.

In Theravāda Buddhist discourses, according to Harvey Aronson two terms are used to define compassion, i.e., *anukampā* and *karuṇā*. Etymologically, "*anukampā*" (which in English, is generally translated as *sympathy*) can be understood as the condition of "being moved" (***kampa***) "in accordance with [others]", or "in response to [other]" (*anu*).[190] It is said to be synonymous with "tender care" (***anuddaya***) and "simple compassion" (*karuṇa*).[191] While the term *karuṇa* (compassion) is derived from the root '*kar*' which means 'to do' or 'to make', and can be understood as that which makes the hearts of good moves at the sufferings of others.[192]

From the above definitions, it looks as if both the terms are synonymous in meaning and usage. But this is not true. According to Aronson, "*karuṇa*" refers to the concern that others be free from suffering and is restricted to specific level of concentration differing from *anukampa* which is also the same concern for others' suffering, but not restricted to any specific level of concentration.[193] And, moreover, the term *karuṇa*, in the Buddhist discourses, is used far less often than the term *anukampa*.[194]

Before proceeding further it is important to note that the notion of *anukampa* and *karuṇa*, as defined by Gotama Buddha himself has much wider and deeper implications than our current understanding of the terms sympathy and compassion. We generally believe that compassion and sympathy simply mean to aid others' material well-being, since we presuppose that a person has only one life to live, and thus our main concern should be to make it pleasurable.[195] But, for Buddha, we are actually trapped in a beginning-less continuum of rebirth – perpetually re-experiencing the sufferings of birth, old age, sickness, and death.[196] So our main aim should be to find a way to escape from this entrapment. And by his teachings, he shows the way to end suffering, which is also an expression of sympathy (*anukampa*) or compassion (*karuṇa*) for the plight of the world.[197]

In Theravāda Buddhism, *karuṇa* appears as one of the four noble virtues or sublime attitude or *brahma-vihāras*.[198] However, it is not clearly defined in discourses; yet, the commentaries and

The Path of Purification do supply definitions and explanations. In *The Path of Purification*, Buddhaghoṣa defines it as that which makes the hearts of the good quiver when others are subjected to suffering or that which dissipates the sufferings of others.[199] Its chief characteristic is the wish to remove the woes of others.[200] In other words, when someone's heart moves, by seeing the suffering of others, to alleviate the suffering with a wish "May they be liberated from their sufferings", then that is *karuṇa*. It has the function of not enduring others' suffering.[201] The meditative cultivation of compassion is particularly effective for counteracting harmlessness.[202]

The above definition makes me explain *karuṇa* under the following two constituents; (1) the sight of suffering, and (2) the subject's reaction.

The sight of suffering is the first constituent of compassion, which differentiates it from other benevolent feelings, like *Metta*.[203] Compassion as mentioned above, is the movement in one's heart by seeing the suffering (or pain) of others, to alleviate the suffering with a wish or a thought "May they be liberated from their sufferings". One would not make such a wish for others if he is not moved by the other's conditions. A person is moved only in those conditions by which he gets deeply affected. And vulnerability of others is one of those conditions, which generally moves the hearts of people. Thus, to arouse compassion, suffering is necessary. And, moreover, in Buddhist teachings suffering has an important place, as it is also illustrated in the Four Noble Truths. The first Noble Truth, *dukkḥa* convey that life is full of suffering. All living beings seek to be free from suffering. But, according to Buddhists, all our ways of trying to reduce suffering, such as possession of wealth, madness for flame or glory or for love etc. offer only a temporary comfort. All these things are impermanent and can leave us worse off, since these things create attachment and envy or suffering for others. The only path that can release us from all these sufferings is in cultivating minds on loving-kindness; and on compassion for self and others.

Here, I think it would be worthy to note that the Buddhist view on suffering is different from Nussbaum's view. Nussbaum believes, as previously mentioned, that in order to have compassion for others, the compassionate-subject must accept a certain picture of the world, a picture according to which the valuable things are not always safely under a person's own control, but liable to damage by fortune. And from this it follows that Nussbaum believes that a human-beings' life is not full of suffering. Suffering is only a little part of human life. A person suffers only on the loss of some valuable things. On the other hand for Buddhists, human life is full of suffering. Even the so-called valuable things or the pleasures gained by these valuable things are fraught with pain and sorrow. Further Nussbaum believes that compassion is an important emotion, as it aids the material well-being of others. But for Buddhists, compassion helps oneself and others to get a relief from the entrapment of all sufferings.

The second constituent of compassion is the reaction of compassionate-subject, i.e., reaction of one's heart by seeing the suffering of others. We can understand this reaction by answering the following questions; (a) What kind of reaction is this?, (b) Why this reaction is necessary?, (c) How does it happen?[204]

(a) This reaction can be understood in terms of empathy accompanied with the thought or wish that "May others be free from their sufferings". And this can happen only when the compassionate-subject possesses the sensibility towards others' sufferings.

Here, it is important to point out that empathizing with others, i.e., feeling the suffering of others does not mean producing sorrow for one's own-self. As maintained by Buddhaghoṣa, 'compassion is characterized as promoting the aspect of allaying suffering. Its function resides in not bearing others' suffering.[205] Here, Buddhaghoṣa adds that compassion succeeds "when it makes cruelty subside and it fails when it produces sorrow"[206]. Like Aristotle,[207] Buddhists do not suggest that it is only through becoming sorrowful ourselves that we are truly compassionate to others.[208] Here one might object that not feeling for others' pain is a symbol of heartlessness. But for the Buddhist it is not heartlessness. 'Between heartlessness, on the one hand, and being thoroughly overwhelmed by others' difficulties, on the other, there lies the option of care without grief. The practitioner must be ever alert to remove any sadness that arises during cultivation of compassion.'[209]

(b) This reaction is necessary as a person being indifferent from the object's suffering can't make a wish for him. And compassion without wish is incomplete.

(c) Now comes the question about how this reaction happens. As stated above, for the reaction to occur, it is important that the subject feels the suffering of others. And, in order to know or feel the suffering of the other, one needs to stand in a relationship with that being. i.e., compassion assumes a relationship or we can say that it is a relational phenomenon. This relationship can be understood by the following verse:

All are frightened of being hurt or of any threat to one's life.

To all, life is dear.

Seeing that others feel the same way as one-self, equating others to oneself, refrain from harming or killing.[210]

There are two ways in which this verse can be interpreted: first, that this verse is emphasizing the concept of comparison; second, that it's emphasizing on the capacity of equalizing our-self with others, which springs from loving-kindness (*Metta*).[211]

If we see this above verse in a literal sense than it follows that one can feel the suffering of others by comparing himself with others. In other words, all human-beings are alike; others feel the same way as one-self. Thus one can know the feeling of other by comparing them to one's own-self. If one concentrates on this meaning then compassion follows from the sensitivity to our own fears and the ability to place ourselves in other's shoes.[212] But this interpretation makes the compassion a self-centered notion as here compassion would be restricted to the subject's own thinking or fears. That is, the subject will be compassionate towards only those cases which he is fearful of.

Second, the term 'equating' can also be understood as 'equalizing'. It is not a comparison where we simply see one-self alike to other people. Here, equalizing moreover means identification of oneself with all beings.[213] For Buddhists, this 'equalization' is grounded on the concept of *metta*[214] (loving-kindness), which is not some passionate love but is rather unconditional love for all beings. Here, love is not bound by any kind of attachment or desire for the other. It (love) is a mental-attitude of closeness, which develops not on the bases of whether someone is close to me, or good to me or not, but rather its bases are with the recognition that the other one is also suffering like me and wants freedom from this suffering. In simple words, here the feeling of love is unbiased and has no hindrance of attachment. To those who object that love is impossible without attachment, the Theravāda tradition answers with a subtle psychological analysis of the nature of a desirous and wholesome state of mind.[215] Attachment always occurs with a lack of clarity, a lack of mental peace, and a disregard for what is most helpful to oneself and others[216]. The absence of attachment does not preclude love. Love (*metta*) is a motivation of compassion. Briefly saying, for the Buddhist, unconditional love is a relationship on which compassion is based.

Furthermore, it is a selfless act because it promotes the happiness of others without expecting a favor in return. We have already seen above that it is helpful action which reduces the suffering of others and also noticed that it promotes the aspect of allaying suffering, manifests non-cruelty, does not produce sorrow and it is liberating action.

Now let us analyze that why it is called a divine abiding and a measureless state by Buddhists.

Buddhaghoṣa maintains that 'the divineness of the abiding (*brahmaviharata*) should be understood here in the sense of best and in the sense of immaculate. For these abiding are the best in being the right attitude towards beings. And just as Brahma gods abide with immaculate minds, so the mediators who associate themselves with these are abiding are on an equal footing with Brahma gods. So they are called divine abiding in the sense of best and in the sense of immaculate.'[217] In simple words, compassion liberates one's mind from all evil-doings, as it is a right attitude towards all-beings. In this sense it makes practitioner's mind neat and clean, i.e., immaculate, like Brahma God.

It is also known as measureless state, for when developed to a high degree in meditation, they are said to make the mind 'immeasurable,' like the mind of loving Brahma god.[218] That is why it is said:

> Their number is due to paths to purity
>
> And other sets of four; their order to their aim

As welfare and the rest. Their scope is found to be Immeasurable, so "measureless states" their name.[219]

These above lines suggest that compassion is an immeasurable state because of its immeasurable scope or the object of compassion being immeasurable. It is focused on the welfare of immeasurable living beings. Buddhists in general believe that each sentient being are one and the same in not liking suffering and pain; there is no difference between any humans whether they are billionaires or beggars, or for that matter any human being or in a small insect. For the Buddhist, unlike for Aristotle, compassion is not restricted towards only few people whom we love, or whom we know, or who are similar to us, but it is a feeling towards immeasurable people, or immeasurable living beings. How this feeling is extended towards all living being, is yet another question, which I will be discussing in subsequent sections.

Is compassion developed or it is based on Our Instincts

As I mentioned above, in Buddhist discourses two terms are used to describe the feeling of compassion: *karuṇa* and *anukampa*. Both the terms are semantic, yet usages of both the terms are distinct. *anukampa* is the fraternal concern that is present in an individual.[220] It does not require cultivation or meditative development.[221] In other words, people require no experience in meditation to have a sense of this attitude. On the other hand, *karuṇa* requires cultivation or meditative development. Fourfold instructions are given for its development.[222]

Sympathy involves wishing for others. For example Gotama lists five practices by which monks are sympathetic to laypersons: 'establishing them in correct conduct; bringing them to a religious outlook; inspiring them to practice mindfulness when they are sick; announcing to them the arrival of monks and thus making them aware of the opportunity to create merits; and eating whatever food they get and thus not getting frustrated by their gifts of confidence'.[223] On the other hand, the teaching of compassion involves cultivation of this attitude in meditation. In simple words, its (compassion) teaching entails only cultivation of the wish that others be free from suffering.[224] Aronson writes, "Though Gotama never articulated a link between the meditation on compassion and subsequent activity on behalf of others, it can be assumed that the cultivation of these attitudes would affect the nature and scope of a meditator's manifest fraternal activity. A practitioner developing concentrated universal compassion would be deeply moved to help a wide range of individuals, without exception."[225]

From this it follows that compassion is an act, which can be developed by practice. In *Visuddhimagga*, Buddhaghoṣa maintained that 'one who wants to develop compassion should begin his task by reviewing the danger in lack of compassion and the advantage in compassion'. first of all, on seeing a wretched man, unlucky, unfortunate, in every way a fit object for compassion, unsightly, reduced to utter misery, with hands and feet cut off, sitting in the shelter for the helpless with a pot placed before him, with a mass of maggots oozing from his arms and legs, and moaning, compassion should be felt for him in this way: "this being has indeed been reduced to misery; if only he could be freed from this suffering."

He further maintains that if he does not encounter such a person, then he can arouse compassion for an evil-doing person, even though he is happy, by comparing him to one about to be executed. How?

'Suppose a robber has been caught with stolen goods, and in accordance with the king's command to execute him, the king's men bind him and lead him off to the place of execution, giving him a hundred blows in sets of four. Then people give him things to chew and eat and also garlands and perfumes, unguents and betel leaves. Although he goes along eating and enjoying these things as though he were happy and well off, still no one fancies that he is really happy and well off. On the contrary people feel compassionate for him, thinking, "this poor wretch is now about to die; every step he takes brings him nearer to the presence of death." So too a *bhikṣu* whose meditation subject is compassion should arouse compassion for an [evil-doing] person even if he is happy: "though this poor wretch is now happy, cheerful, enjoying his wealth, still for want of even one good deed done now in any one of the three doors [of body, speech and mind] he can come to experience untold suffering in the states of loss."'[226]

After having aroused compassion for this kind of person, he should next cultivate it for a dear person, then for a neutral person, and then for a hostile person, successively in the same way.[227]

In the beginning meditation towards the wretched and unlucky is instructed, and this might be done from the point of easier cultivation because with this kind of object there is a greater equanimity. Then object of meditation shifts towards an offender who is happy but going to be punished, for we easily feel for such a kind of man who is unaware of or ignorant about his own vulnerable condition. Here, one thing would also seem to be important enough to note down, that for Buddhists, compassion is all pervasive. It is not restricted even to those persons who deserve the punishment.[228] Then object of meditation shifts towards dear ones, and the one towards whom subject is indifferent, for the obvious reason that we easily feel for such kind of persons. When one feels compassion towards them as same as the compassion he feels toward one's friends and relative, then one meditates on compassion for all sentient beings throughout all the directions of the universe in same way. Here it is important to see that in Buddhism compassion is very centered on the individual practicing. It is developed through meditation.

It must be remembered that for Buddhists compassion is not directed only towards other-beings. Practice of compassion for one's own self is also emphasized. Self-compassion is not some selfish self-love out of self-possession, but it has a deeper meaning. It means being aware of our own suffering, and taking care of our own self as we take care of other-beings. The main aim of the Buddhist is to get freedom and also liberate others from this worldly entrapment. And toward this aim compassion is directed. Buddhists believes that to get freedom for one self, one must be compassionate towards their own sufferings.

Purpose of Compassion

Being practical philosophers, Buddhists do not confine themselves to the definition of compassion, they also explain the purpose of it.

Buddhaghoṣa, in *Vissudhimagga*, maintains that compassion has a fixed purpose. Its purpose is to ward off cruelty,[229] so that one could achieve the bliss of insight and an excellent [from of future] existence.[230] It also brings a state of peace for the mind, since the development of it plays an essential part in the meditation practice that leads towards inward calm.[231] The excellent existence[232] rests on it because it has the power to weaken the defilements of lust, ill-will, and delusion. In short compassion by reducing the suffering of others and also by reducing the suffering of one's own self brings peace and harmony. It also liberates one's minds from the power of destructive emotions such as lust, ill-will (anger, envy and vengeance), delusion (all kinds of fear) and brings inward clam.

From the above account the following characteristics of compassion can be comprehended;

1. It is 'a selfless act', i.e., Altruistic in nature.

Buddhist maintains that compassion is altruistic in nature, because it compels one to serve others and himself with altruistic motives. A truly compassionate person lives not only for himself but for others. He seeks opportunities to serve others expecting nothing in return, not even gratitude. He does not make distinction between living-creatures. He extends his compassion without any distinction to all living beings, even to oneself and one's foe. The ideal of practice, for him, is to selflessly act to alleviate suffering wherever it appears.

2. It promotes the aspect of allaying suffering.

Compassion is not only a fellow-feeling for others' plight, but it also a response where one makes wishes or act to dissipates the suffering of himself and others.

3. It manifests non-cruelty.

For the Buddhist, compassion is opposite of cruelty. It is based on loving-kindness.

4. It does not produce sorrow.

Here the feeling of compassion, unlike Aristotle and Aquinas does not include sorrow or suffering on the part of its subject. Instead, for the Buddhist, compassion brings inward calm, since it liberates one's mind from lust, ill-will and delusion.

5. It is deliverance of mind and a liberating action.

It liberates mind from destructive emotions (lust, ill-will, delusion).

6. It is called divine abiding and Measureless state.

For Buddhists, compassion is all pervasive. It pervades even one's foe. It is also not restricted even to those persons who deserve the punishment.

From all the above discussions the following analysis can be made:

According to Buddhists, compassion is a fellow-feeling which does not involves feeling of pain or sorrow. But here a question arises; is it really possible to have compassion for others without feeling any kind of pain? Compassion by its very definition means 'feeling with the sufferer', as we have already discussed. When one says that he/she is feeling with the sufferer, then it implies that he/she is sharing some kind of suffering of the sufferer. And 'feeling suffering' itself means that the person is experiencing some kind of pain or sorrow. This question seems like a puzzle to us, but it might not be problematic to Buddhist practitioners.

In Buddhism, compassion is limitless; it is extended on all types of suffering. Unlike Nussbaum, here compassion is not limited to only serious kind of sufferings. Buddhists believe that 'life is full of suffering (dukkha)'. Even the so-called pleasures are fraught with pain and sorrow. And the aim of overcoming *dukkha* is the central preoccupation of them, and one towards which compassion contributes. Two points thus stands out:

1. That since all existence is suffering, compassion is all encompassing rather than being episodic.
2. That compassion can be cultivated as a state of mind during meditation.

To sum up, it seems that compassion for Buddhists is both a virtue and an emotion. In the above sections it is described in two ways; first as *anukampā* and second as *karuṇā*. *anukampā* is an inbuilt feeling. And from this it follows that it is moreover like some instinctive emotion, with which men are born. While *karuṇā* is defined as a quality which can be developed. Men are not born with this quality, but they develop this through practice or meditation. Since it can be developed and it can be defined as a virtue.

Nature of Compassion in Sikhism

Compassion plays a key role in the ethics of Sikhs. In Gurumukhi, the term *dayā* is generally used to denote compassion. *dayā*, which usually spelt "*daia*" in Punjabi, is a borrowed term. It is borrowed from a Sanskrit word *dayā* meaning to have sympathies with, to have pity on. But it is more positive and deeper in sentiment than what is usually meant by the word sympathy.[233] *Dayā* means suffering in the suffering of other's beings. Cognitively, it observes the other's pain; affectively, it gets touched by it and moves with affectionate responses for the sufferer.[234] Here, compassion is the willingness to help the other being who is suffering.

Sikh texts generally express *dayā* in two senses: first, as compassion and second, as a quality of God.[235] Satnaam Kaur in *Three Basics of Sikh Religious Thought* also defines the term (*dayā*) as having two important ways, i.e., compassion and redress.[236] The former term, she asserts, defines *dayā* as an impulsion to relieve a person's distress, melting of the heart.[237] It is not a passive feeling, but it is an empathic altruism that actively strives to free others from suffering. And the latter defines it (*dayā*) as an act or quality of God providing assistance or relief to men in various ways.[238] In this chapter, my main attempt will be to examine the concept of *dayā* with reference to Satnaam Kaur's first sense–as an impulsion, wanting others to be free from suffering. For this purpose, I would confine myself to the study of the Ādi Granth and Janam Sākhis.

In the first part of this section I would discuss my reason for selecting the Ādi Granth and Janam Sākhis for the development of this chapter. And, in the next part I would discuss the nature of compassion as a moral mentioned in Janam-Sākhis. Here my study is not only focused on the morals as they ought to be practiced according to the teachings of the *Gurus*, but also a study of morals as actually practiced by the Sikhs. After this, I would proceed to the discussion of compassion according to the Ādi Granth.

Why *Ādi Granth* and *Janam Sākhis*?

Ādi Granth and Janam Sākhis are the two important sources to determine the nature of compassion in Sikh literatures. Ādi Granth or *Guru Granth Sahib*[239] is the principle scripture of the Sikhs, complied in 1604 by *Guru Arjan Dev.*[240] This scripture is contained in a volume of fourteen hundred thirty pages, comprising of a collection of the writings of *Gurus* and some other *Bhagats* (saints), and is written in more than one language. The medium used by the *Gurus* in this scripture is poetry and the master poets have also kept in mind the rhythm along the thought-content.[241] I have chosen Ādi Granth for the following reasons. Firstly, it is the most authentic work of Sikhism, personally contributed by *Gurus*. Secondly, it is comprehensive in nature. Thirdly, it consolidates the ethics of the Sikhs, since it lays a great stress on moral conduct or praxis. It revolves around the socio-natural environment of men. Avtar Singh also maintains that the Ādi Granth is full of ethico-spiritual insights of *Gurus*, as the *Gurus* were men of vision.[242] According to him, there are three cardinal themes of the Ādi Granth, i.e., man, society of man and man in union with the spiritual entity. In this way, the teachings of Ādi Granth were sensitive to the socio-natural environments of man.[243]

The Janam Sākhis which literally mean birth-evidence are hagiographic accounts of the *Gurus*, each consisting of a series of chapters, or incidents, called sākhis. Gurmukhi is used as the script for all the important Janam-Sākhis, but the language may be either Punjabi or the composite dialect called *sadhukkari* or *sant-bhāṣā*.[244] There are some questions concerning the authenticity of the Janam-Sākhis. As W. H. Mcleod points out, "the problem as far as the *Janam-Sakhis* are concerned is to determine how much of their material can be accepted as historical."[245] But this concern is not an enough reason to neglect the authenticity of Janam-Sākhis, as Mcleod further wrote, "in spite of their manifest short-comings we are bound to rely on the Janam-Sākhis for almost all our information concerning these events (events of *Gurus'* life), for there is nothing to replace them and little to supplement them."[246]

I have selected Janam Sākhis for the following reasons. Firstly, Janam Sākhis are an important source for a beginner. In these Janam Sākhis the eye of the narrator is always on the moral or the practical lesson to which these anecdotes invariably lead.[247] As Avtar Singh writes, "It is through the tales of Gurus' life that the young children and the lay are nurtured and introduced to the ethical precepts of Sikhism. Herein are told the many morals like altruism, compassion and social services that enrich the man's moral life."[248] Thus, we can easily find a strong message of compassion within these stories. Secondly, it is a study of the morals as actually practiced by the Sikhs. As Avtar Singh writes, the Janam Sākhis by virtue of their very nature, scope and methodology do not attempt at building any ethical system, though they themselves preserve a vivid record of values and morals cherished during the time of the *Gurus*.[249]

This is a textual study of the original sources to discover the nature of compassion and its role in Sikh ethics. Here one thing is important to consider that in Ādi Granth the ethical teachings are intertwined with the metaphysical and religious declarations. The renowned Sikh scholar Avtar Singh, in his book *Ethics of the Sikhs* writes, "This is done for the simple reason that in actual life itself a person finds them comingled."[250] But, in this research, I will try to separate or extract the ethical nature of compassion from the metaphysical declarations given in the Ādi Granth and Janam Sākhis.

Lastly, it is still a raw subject-matter to deal with philosophically and hence has presented difficulties.

Compassion in *Janam-Sakhis*

There are many stories in the *Janam-Sakhis* which are a portrayal of compassion. It is neither possible, nor within the scope of the present task, to reproduce all of them here. For the present purpose, I have selected two of such stories, which have been there for centuries and can well represent the Sikh ideology.

The first one is from Bhai Bālā's *Janam-Sakhi* of Guru Nanak[251]. This story is famously known as *Sacha Soda*.

It is a story of Nanak, when he was about 16 years of age............. One day his father Kalu gave him twenty silver rupees and asked to invest the sum usefully. He advised him to purchase goods from the neighboring market town of *Chuharkana*, which he could sell at a profit. ....In a jungle that lay on the way, Nanak fell in with a large party of bare-skinned *sādhus* who had been without food for several days. Some of these were so much into speculation that they were unaware of their body's bad condition. Nanak felt distressed and ....marched on to the town of *Chuharkana*, and......spent there the entire sum on provisions for the hungry men in the forest. With supplies of wheat flour, sugar and ghee he hurried back to the spot where he had left them....father

Kalu was angry at his son for doing such a deed. He asked from him in the harshest terms, why did he do this. To this Nanak politely answered, "Father, you asked me to invest the sum usefully, and there could be none other way to invest it usefully."[252]

The moral outline of this story is that we should help others when and wherever we can. By this Guru Nanak taught the people in a simple and direct way, the true message of compassion, i.e., help others without taking care of own profit.

The second story is from the life of Bhai Kanhaiya.[253] He was a contemporary of ninth and tenth *Gurus.*

During Guru Gobind Singh's time many wars were being waged to protect the innocents. During the war of Anadpur, Bhai Kanhaiya was ordered to serve water to his own wounded people. But the suffering of wounded enemies moved him and he served water to the friends and the foes, to conscious and unconscious one indiscriminately. But this act of compassion stirred up criticism amongst his fellow Sikhs,[254] and they lodged a complaint against him to Guru Gobind Singh. The Guru called him and asked for his explanation against the charge. Bhai Kanhiya bowed and submitted, "My Lord! Ever since I touched your lotus feet, I do not differentiate between man and man. I see thy image in every one. Thou hast so enlightened my eyes that I see no one else other than thee. I see thy all pervading divine spirit everywhere and in all. I serve none else but thee my lord, and to thee only I served. It is thee who taught me:-

"Listen my eyes! To you has the Lord granted light,
Nothing beside him behold,
Beside the Lord, nothing behold,
By His grace Him I beheld,

This poison-Laden world that you behold,
In it is Beheld the divine image,
By the Mater's grace has this realization come,
Whenever I look, God alone I see,
Nothing but God is visible,
Saint Nanak, blind of sight were my eyes,
By the holy Preceptor's touch.
Have they found illuminated vision.[255]

From the time I had the Guru's company,
All the jealously I have forgotten,
None to me is my foe or alien,
Friendly to all I am.[256]

The Guru was extremely pleased with the spirit of all embracing love and self-less service exhibited by Bhai Kanhaiya. He applauded him for his humanitarian and compassionate service and for understanding the deep message of Gurbani. He appreciated him and offered him a box of ointment for proving first-aid to the wounded.[257]

This story is primarily about the devotion, but has an explicit message of compassion also. The hidden moral of this story is that one should be compassionate to all irrespective of who the sufferer is. In other words, one should help even to one's foe. In this story, the main indication is towards compassion in the sense of universal brotherhood.[258]

Both stories have a deep message of compassion or self-less service. From these above stories the following sketch about the nature of compassion can be drawn.

1. Compassion is a feeling of distress or pain aroused by seeing the suffering of others with an impulse to relieve them, as in both stories the narrator feels distress when he encounters the other's pain. It seems that it is some kind of psychological pain.
2. These two stories also indicate that compassion can be felt for those who are unaware of their sufferings. As in the first story the narrator feels compassion for those *sa dhus* also who were not conscious of their hunger. And in the second story the narrator served water to unconscious persons as well. Here one might see similarities between Nussbaum's notion and the view of Sikhism, i.e., both maintain that compassion can be felt for those who are unaware of their suffering. But other than this the Sikh account of compassion is quite distinct from Nussbaum's account. Unlike Nussbaum, Sikhism does not believe that compassion is restricted to those who have created the suffering for themselves, as very-well depicted in both the above stories. In the second story, the narrator shows compassion to his enemies also, who have caused suffering for themselves. Although, like Nussbaum, Sikhism to some extent also maintains that the subject of compassion judges the seriousness of suffering, as follows from both the above stories, but unlike Nussbaum, the subject of compassion does not judge the level of seriousness in a strict sense. According to Sikhism, a compassionate subject will show compassion to every one who is suffering, without really judging the level of seriousness. Here compassion is not only a response towards serious suffering. Compassion in Sikhism is

extended towards everyone. Whether the object's suffering seems serious to the subject or not, or whether the object of compassion is aware of their suffering or not.

3. Additionally this feeling is not limited towards any particular set of people, as maintained by Aristotle.[259] It is limitless, and extended even towards one's foe.
4. Here the stress is on the action of help, unlike Aristotle's definition[260] where no attention is given to action. Not only in these tales but also in the preaching of Ādi Granth great attention is given to the 'action of help', which I will discuss in the next section.
5. Our ability to love others, i.e., the feeling of universal brotherhood, makes other's suffering real to us and facilitates our benevolent desires for the other's good. Here, the feeling of brotherhood plays a key role in achieving an understanding of others distress or pain. In Sikhism it is believed that the whole of humanity is bound by a fraternal relationship.[261] It is a strict instruction of the *Gurus* that all ought to treat every one else as equal, belonging to one reality.[262]

Compassion in *Ādi Granth* or *Guru Granth Sahib*

The Ādi Granth which is a primary scripture of the believers of Sikhism provides instruction to ardent learners for their problem-laden journey of life. It teaches many virtues which help them to become better persons and a useful member of the saintly society. Compassion (*dAya*) is one of them,[263] which is highly prized by all *Gurus.* The importance of compassion can be seen from the following phrases of Ādi Granth:

The mythical bull is dharma, the son of compassion; this is what patiently holds the earth in its place. One who understands this becomes truthful.[264]

This verse provides a simple but an important guide to all believers to follow the path of compassion in their daily lives to become righteous. It is believed that the sanctity of this world is held in place by *dharma* (path of righteousness). And through a simile of the bull (of *dharma*) the son of compassion, Guru Nanak tries to emphasize the importance of compassion. He wants to point out that the path of righteousness can be found only by practicing compassion.

Other verses might also be quoted to show the importance of compassion;

You have no compassion; the Lord's light does not shine in you. You are drowned, drowned in worldly entanglements.[265]

i.e., Compassion is the key of getting liberation from the worldly entanglements.

The mind has entered this cave. It does not leave this cave to wander in the ten directions. Knowing their Lord and Master, people show compassion; then, they become immortal, and attain the state of eternal dignity.[266] //8//

i.e., only when people show the compassion to other sentient beings do they get freedom.

In these above verses compassion is mentioned as an important activity of attaining liberation. It is the chief method or an important means to attain spiritual growth.

There is no systematic exposition about the meaning of the term compassion in Sikh scriptures. It might be that the need for such an exposition was not felt during the life-time of the *Gurus*. But, besides this fact, we can trace the meaning of term compassion in various sayings of *Gurus*.

How can anyone know the pain of the other, if there is no compassion and sympathy within?[267]

Compassion appears to signify an ability to feel others' pain. As maintained above, only by having compassion one would be able to perceive the pain of others.

Beholding the sight of petitioner, compassion is not aroused. No one lives without give and take.[268]

Compassion also appears not a passive feeling, but an active one. In other words, compassion is not only a feeling of sympathy by seeing the sight of suffering; it involves the action of help. It is incomplete without action, as depicted in the above verse. In Sikhism, compassion conveys no meaning without an action of help. Thus it shows that for Sikhs, help is a necessary factor of compassion. It is generally believed in Sikhism that 'If someone needs food or clothes or is needy otherwise, share your earning with him. If somebody needs your help, do not tarry, leave your own work and go for his help.'[269] But, from here we should not conclude that compassion without action of help is not possible in Sikhism. To make it clearer let us look at the following example; suppose a person has seen news on Television that group of five people is stuck in a storm in an Atlantic sea. There is a no way to help them or save them. Here a question arises that 'is compassion possible for these kinds of cases in Sikhism?' In my understanding, Sikhism would answer in an affirmative way. According to Sikhism, we can show our compassion for these people by offering prayers for them.

The Next line states;

Through compassion, the naked hermit reflects upon his inner self. He slays his own self, instead of slaying others.[270]

i.e., when one practices compassion he lets go on his ego.

Even if someone practices such self-discipline, compassion and devotional worship – if he is filled with greed, and his mind is engrossed in corruption, how can he find the immaculate Lord?[271]

i.e., compassion can not exist with vices like greed and corruption. Practice of compassion presumes demolishing of such vices in one's mind and habits.

Here virtue can be defined as a quality exhibited in right conduct.[272] And compassion by its very nature exhibits itself as part of right conduct, as it is altruistic in nature. When one practices compassion he sacrifices his own ego, instead of sacrificing others, as stated in the above verse. From these lines it follows that compassion is a morally perfect virtue, which can't exist with vices like greed and corruption. In this way, here also compassion is a way to purify one's own mind, as in Buddhism. It is the best way to reflect upon one's own self. Here one thing is important to note that it is not necessary that compassion always contains the element of altruism. It may or it may not contain altruism. It is the situation that helps to define altruism – like the sacrifice of Guru Teghbhadur to rescue *Kasmiri pandits.*[273]

From the above it is clear that compassion is a feeling of pain accompanied with an act of help. It is also clear that it is not a bare emotion but a virtue.[274] But if it is a virtue then the next question arises; 'Is it infused in one or can be developed by practice?' To say that a virtue is infused is to say that God is responsible for it; it is a gift of God.

In Sikh scripture, compassion is treated both as a gift of God and a skill which can be learnt. This can be more clearly seen in the following verses preached by *Gurus*;

Compassion, righteousness, Dharma and intense meditation are eternal and imperishable; they alone obtain these, who have such pre-ordained destiny.[275]

i.e., the quality of compassion is eternal and imperishable. And one is born with this quality.

He alone obtains meditation, austerities, self-discipline, compassion and Dharmic faith, whom the Lord so blesses.[276]

i.e., compassion is a gift of God.

Truth, contentment, compassion, Dharmic faith and purity – I have received these from the teachings of the saints. Says Nanak, one who realizes this in his mind, achieves total understanding.[277]

In this verse Guru Nanak is pointing out that he himself receives the quality of compassion from the teachings of the saints. Thus it can be said that quality of compassion can be developed.

Following the Guru's Teachings, compassion and contentment are found.[278]

i.e., compassionate behavior can be learnt.

These above verses portray compassion as God's gift, but it does not mean that it can't be developed. It can be learnt through the teachings of *Gurus* and practical experiences. Since it is acknowledged as a virtue,[279] it can be developed. According to Ādi Granth, the virtues may be learnt and cultivated through social communication with the virtuous. This is very well brought out by Guru Nanak, he says, "In the society of the holy, one becomes holy, and runs after virtues, forsaking his sins."[280] And at yet another place he remarks, "If my friends are blessed with virtues, let us share some with them. Yes, share we should the virtues with our friends and shed our sins."[281]

In this brief survey of literature relating to the Sikh's conception of compassion, the following analysis can be made. First, compassion is a fellow-feeling that arises on seeing the suffering of the other accompanied with a wish or an action of help. Second, it is not an emotion but a virtue, a quality exhibited in right conduct, which can be learnt. Third, the relation between the sufferer and one who is showing compassion is only established by unconditional love (on behalf of the subject). But besides these facts, some questions are left unanswered in this discussion. It is said that compassion is focused on the suffering of the others, but the criteria of knowing the sufferings of the others is not described, as it is described by Aristotle, Aquinas and others. And second, the method of developing love is also not clearly discussed, as mentioned by the Buddhists. These questions may sound unacceptable to the believer but, I think, it is worthwhile to refer to them here. We do not find any such discussions in Sikh-literature. The absence of such an attempt could have been inspired by the feeling that discussions of such issues are not necessary. It could also be due to the presuppositions of *Gurus'* teachings as we know that the virtue of compassion is based on love and it is not some sensuous love, but love without qualifications.

Another question arises: It is said that compassion can be learnt through teaching of *Gurus*, by keeping company of compassionate people. Does this mean it is only an imitation? Or, 'Does it mean that one naturally absorbs the good quality and this becomes habitual?' How can an imitated act be an act of compassion in the true sense? I believe that the inculcation of good qualities here does not mean only imitating the virtuous one or the *Guru's* qualities.

It means absorbing the *Guru's* qualities by regular practices, by making the *Guru* a role-model.

Compassion-Cases

I now come back to my original question about the nature of compassion. I take up the same cases (of Martha Nussbaum and Brain Carr) to analyze how the Buddhists and Sikhs would respond to them.

The first example that Nussbaum took up was the *loss of reason*: of a person who altogether lost the use of reason. For Nussbaum, this man is an object of compassion to all.[282]

The second example is of the *Peacocks' tongues.* 'Q, a Roman aristocrat, discovers that his shipment of peacocks' tongues has been interrupted. Feeling that his dinner party that evening will be a total disaster in consequence, he weeps bitter tears, and implores his friend Seneca to pity him. Seneca laughs'.[283]

The third example is of the deprivation of the uneducated women. Nussbaum takes the example of a woman (R) in rural India, who is severely under-nourished and poorly educated, but has no idea of what it is to feel healthy and also no idea of the benefits and pleasures of education. This woman does not even think that her lot is a bad one. But, on the others hand, hearing about her many others feel deeply moved to render help.[284]

The fourth example I took up was given by Brain Carr of a professional solider who in his enthusiasm suffered horrific injuries and is carried off to the field hospital. Here, the fault was his own, but humanity calls sympathy for his suffering.[285] According to Carr, we cannot just turn away and reject this soldier as a fool. If so then we would be imposing our value system upon him.[286]

The first three examples are given by Nussbaum and the fourth one is given by Carr to criticize Nussbaum's position. Their positions, as described in the last chapter, are as follows: Nussbaum, like Aristotle, believes that compassion involves a recognition that something bad has happened with someone.[287] She named this a 'judgment of size.'[288] She insisted that it is the subject (the onlooker) who judges the seriousness of the situation.[289] And by first three examples she tried to show that we generally feel compassion for those cases where we judge the suffering is serious. But according to Carr, Nussbaum's thesis that one who feels compassion is the judge of seriousness cannot be supported by the very definition of compassion. He asserts that compassion by its very definition involves a shared experience of suffering[290]. He called this experience of shared suffering a 'felt suffering.'[291] He maintained that if the sufferer's suffering is unfelt then there would be no room for a sympathetic response other than pity.[292] Compassion can only be felt on those cases where the subject feels with the sufferer. The loss of reason and the uneducated deprivation case are both examples of unfelt suffering, here the subject can't feel with the sufferer, that's why in these cases only pity can be felt, over shadowing the feeling of compassion. On the other hand, the case of Peacock's tongue is an example of felt suffering, and for this simple reason, here, the subject can feel compassion for the sufferer.[293]

The above discussion reveals that, for Nussbaum and Carr, compassion is restricted by certain limits. As we have already discussed that for Nussbaum it is restricted by personal judgment, and for Carr it is restricted by experience of felt suffering. But it is quite interesting to know that in Sikhism and Buddhism compassion is not limited by any such limits. A Buddhist and a Sikh will show compassion to all, first without judging the seriousness of the plight, and second, by showing compassion even to those people who are unaware of their sufferings.

And as far as these above examples are concerned, I think an agent would deal with the first three cases in the following way. Like Nussbaum, a Buddhist and a Sikh will show compassion to the person who lost the use of reason, i.e., who is not able to feel his suffering. But, like Nussbaum, this agent does not feel compassion for the victim only because of his personal judgments or restricted notions, but because of his feeling of unconditional love for the sufferer.

Further, like Nussbaum, the Buddhists would show their compassion for R not only because she lacks some luxuries, but because she is trapped in the cycle of birth and death.

As far as the reply of Sikhism is concerned, I think, they would not show compassion for R. Here one can object by posing a question that if according to Sikhism in the 'loss of reason' case situation compassion is justified, then why isn't it in this case? A 'loss of reason' means either a person is unconscious (e.g., coma stage) or has lost the capability of reasoning (e.g., psychological problems). Sikhism would show compassion for both the persons, i.e., for the unconscious one and for the one who has lost reasoning capability, because in these cases victims are not conscious, they are not in a stage that they could comprehended their suffering. But in case of R, R (a rural woman) is fully conscious. She is able to feel and comprehend her situation. As we know, in this case, R is not feeling bad for her own condition, and for this simple reason one can not suffer with her.

As far as the case of Q is concerned, it is difficult to find an answer to how a Buddhist and a Sikh would respond. Let's see first what the problem is in this case. Q is a rich person who has lost his shipment of peacocks' tongue. And now he is sad because his dinner is going to get spoilt as its consequences. According to Nussbaum, compassion is not possible in such cases. Here one might think that since Q is feeling sad and compassion means feeling with the sufferer, the latter is justified. But this example is not so easy. The ethical concern for the peacock, which has been killed for the dinner party, is also involved. Killing in itself is an ethical-crime.

But does this mean that we should not show compassion to those who kill and eat animals. Many people would help the man who is in pain due to the chicken bone stuck in his throat. For non-vegetarians chicken is an edible-thing like plants. Similarly if we take the peacock as an edible-thing, than we might feel compassionate for Q. But if the Buddhists and the Sikhs will show compassion for Q, than it is because of their wider understanding of suffering, and not because they are taking the peacock only as an edible-thing. It is because they have learnt the habit of unconditional love; love to all without discrimination. For both, the relation between the sufferer and the one who is feeling compassion is of unconditional love. And because of the feeling of unconditional love Buddhists and Sikhs respect others and their feelings. They will help others if they are in need.

With the aid of the fourth example, Carr directly criticized Nussbaum's clause of blamelessness. Nussbaum, like Aristotle, maintains that we do not feel compassion for those people who have created suffering for themselves. But according to Carr, we generally feel compassion even for those cases where the subject brings suffering on themselves, as shown in the forth example. He asserts that we know the fault was the soldiers', but humanity demanded an appreciation of his suffering.[294] Like Carr, in this case, Buddhism and Sikhism would not restrict their compassion towards those who themselves created suffering.

Overview

This chapter reveals the essence of compassion by looking at how Theravāda Buddhism and Sikhism use and describe this term. Discussion of both philosophies reveals that compassion is a fellow-feeling, which is based on unconditional love and always accompanied with a desire to relieve the sufferer. This discussion also shows that the views of Buddhism and Sikhism differ from each others regarding the question of the 'subject's suffering'. Buddhists believe that compassion does not involve suffering for the subject, while from the discussion on Sikhism, compassion appears to involve suffering for the subject as well.

This chapter also shows that for Buddhism and Sikhism, compassion is not only a response towards the serious issues but it is extended also towards non-serious issues. Moreover, Buddhists describe the unique concept of compassion for oneself and one's meditative development. They clearly describe the way its can be enhanced and also describe its practical purpose. On the other hand the discussion in Sikhism about compassion is not so clear on how it is to be developed. Furthermore, this chapter also considers whether compassion is a virtue or an emotion. I show that for Buddhists it is both an emotion and a virtue, but for Sikhism it is a virtue alone.

4

Conclusion

The goal of this research is to examine the nature of compassion by way of a comparative analysis of the philosophy of Aristotle, Aquinas, Nussbaum, Buddhism and Sikhism. My research intended to answer a series of questions as raised in the introduction.

- My first question was whether compassion is the same or distinct from pity, sympathy/empathy, love, or benevolence?
  - ➢ From my discussions it can be concluded that the meaning of compassion is over and above that of pity, sympathy, love or benevolence. Compassion, unlike pity, does not include the feeling of condescension. Sympathy, unlike compassion, does not involve the desire or action of help. Benevolence and love have a wider meaning than compassion does. Love can be taken as a base from which compassion springs, but it is not synonymous with compassion.
- My second question was whether compassion involves sorrow or pain. In other words does the compassionate subject suffer with same intensity as the sufferer.
  - ➢ With the exception of Buddhism, I found that all others accounts (Aristotle, Aquinas, Nussbaum and

Sikhism) I analyzed held that the feeling of compassion involved suffering on the part of its subject. It involved some kind of psychological pain. And the intensity of the suffering varied from case to case, i.e., the compassionate-subject's suffering could be the same or different from that of the sufferer. It depended on the relation by which he got attached to the sufferer.

- The next question I raised was whether compassion was only a response towards serious suffering or was it also a response towards non serious suffering.
  - ➢ For Aristotle and Nussbaum compassion was only a response towards serious suffering, while for Aquinas, Buddhism and Sikhism it is seen it in a wider perspective. For the latter it is a response even towards non-serious suffering. The previous discussion also demonstrates this perspective
- The forth question was to do with whether the compassionate subject made a relationship with the sufferer.
  - ➢ Different kinds of relationships are contended by different philosophers as illustrated throughout my analysis. Among them are the 'capability of remembrance or supposition' (as maintained by Aristotle); 'eudaimonistic judgment' (according to Nussbaum); and unconditional love (for Aquinas, Buddhism and Sikhism).
- Another question was to do with whether compassion was a virtue or an emotion.

- My research saw compassion more like a virtue and less as an emotion. Aristotle asserted that it is an emotion, while the analysis of his account illustrated that it is a virtue. Nussbaum also defined it as an emotion but maintained that it involved reason and choices which are clear characteristics of virtue. For Aquinas and Sikhism, it is a virtue. For Buddhists, it is both an emotion as well as a virtue.

- My next question asked whether compassion is a part of the human instinct or is learnt through practice.
  - The discussion on Buddhism and Sikhism showed that compassion is both a part of human instinct and can be developed as well. Aristotle and Aquinas also maintained that it can be developed. Nussbaum asserted that as an emotion, it is a part of human instinct. But, she added, that compassion is based on eudaimonistic judgment which is itself a result of a person's life-long learning.
- My final question was to do with whether there is or can be a single universal understanding of the term compassion.
  - My analysis showed that there is no universal understanding of the term compassion. Different philosophical claims about compassion reach contrasting conclusions. Many kinds of understandings about the nature of compassion can be discerned from these discussions. Some suggest compassion is only a response towards serious sufferings (Aristotle, Nussbaum); that it requires the blamelessness of the sufferer (Aristotle, Nussbaum); that it requires knowledge of similar possibilities

> (Aristotle); that it requires a 'eudaimonistic judgment' (Nussbaum). While others hold that compassion is a fellow-feeling intertwined with a desire or willingness to relieve the victim (Buddhism and Sikhism). Here, the conception of compassion does not intermingle with the conception of pain or sorrow. And the link between the compassion-feeler and the sufferer is achieved through an unconditional love.

For a closer look, let me critically analyze some of the important requirements of compassion:

I, first, look at the requirement of serious suffering: My overall analysis reveals that compassion arises in response to suffering. Or we can say that there is commonality amongst all philosophical discussions that suffering is the object of compassion. Nussbaum points out that not all kinds of suffering, but only serious sufferings that are central to sufferer's life is an object of compassion. She further argues that it is the subject who judges the seriousness of the suffering. And it is not necessary the object of compassion be aware of his condition.[295]

But I tend to disagree with this slightly. Let us understand this through the following example of 'P' who is person who has suffered some serious misfortune. According to Nussbaum, the compassionate-subject must see P's misfortune in relation to P's well-being, as she believes that we do not generally feel compassionate for someone who has lost a trivial item, such as tooth-brush or a paper clip, or even an important item that is readily replaceable. But I argue that situations might be very different from what we believe them to be. Suppose P is a child who has lost his favorite pen or some favorite toy, gifted by his grandmother. The loss of this pen matters to him more than the compassionate-subject can imagine. This loss might seem trivial to us; as we know this loss is not affecting his overall well-being. But, for him it's a great loss and it really hurts him. Hence, we cannot simply reject his suffering only because the loss seems to be of no value to us. Compassion, as Carr suggests, is 'suffering with the sufferer'[296] and not only suffering on sufferer's plight. That's why here P should be treated as the object of compassion as his suffering is real to him.

To analyze this better, let us look at Nussbaum's example of the uneducated rural women. R, the uneducated rural woman, who has no idea of the benefits of education and is under-nourished, believes that she is living a good and flourishing life. Here, in agreement with Carr, we cannot feel compassion in this case, as it is a case of unfelt-suffering; I also add to this that judging other's conditions, just in the capacity of my limited observances and experiences, would not be fair enough to come to a conclusive assumption. We might look at the women's condition objectively with a perspective of urban comforts, but fail to see the comforts she's happy with. This does not mean that there's no scope of improvement, but neither does it mean that it's a sorry state all together. The underlying thing about compassion is that what the sufferer is feeling matters the most, rather than what compassionate-subject believes about the other's suffering.

My second object of enquiry is to do with the blamelessness requirement: Aristotle and Nussbaum[297] claim that compassion involves blamelessness of the sufferer, that the suffering has not come his way due to the sufferer himself. This claim does not seem to me right for two reasons. The first is, as Carr noted, that sometimes we feel compassion rather than blame or reproach for those who are themselves responsible for their own miserable condition. To prove this, he gives an example of a soldier, who in his enthusiasm brings suffering onto himself, and we yet feel for his suffering. Here again I tend to agree with Carr as I mentioned earlier, that compassion by its very definition is not restricted by such clauses. It transcends the compassionate-subject's personal judgments and understands the negative condition in terms of the object's heart and mind.

Secondly, sometimes the compassionate person does not judge the sufferer's overall condition. For example: X is passing by a road and sees a road accident which happened because of the victim (P's) mistake. X does not know that P himself is responsible for his accident and X moves ahead to help. Hence, it is possible to have compassion for the sufferer in many situations without even judging his overall condition.

But this does not mean that compassion necessarily involves the element of forgiveness or ignorance. It may include it or it may not. For instance, would we be compassionate to a rapist who is responsible for the victims' terrible condition? I think not. Even if the person feels guilty for his act, then too it is difficult to feel compassion for him. Since the very act this person has caused suffering to another.

Another requirement extends to 'similar possibilities': This requirement demands that we accept that the sufferer is like our self and that what is happening to him, can happen to us.[298] I argue that this acceptance is not always required for compassion to occur. For example, I could feel compassion for a schizophrenic person, yet not accept that it could happen to me. And a man may have never been raped, but this does not preclude his experiencing compassion for a rape victim. He can understand, directly or indirectly, from his own experience what it is to feel intense fear, hurt, anger, distrust, and powerlessness. Therefore he can empathize with a rape victim at least to some degree and possibly play an important role in her recovery.

The requirement of 'similar possibilities' rests on the link between compassion and fear. Compassion is not felt by those who have no fear for future, as Aristotle claims, it cannot be felt by those who are completely ruined and believe that they can suffer no further evil, nor by those who imagine themselves to be well off and unassailable. I would rather differ and say that the fear of mishaps is not enough for compassion to happen. Consider the example of a young unmarried man who is suffering from some serious disease. He knows that he is going to die within a few days. This man believes that now nothing worse could befall him. But when he sees the suffering of a man who has lost his dear wife and child in some accident, he is moved, despite the fact that the chances of this kind of suffering happening to him are negligible.

Another requirement of compassion can be identified as eudaimonistic judgment: Nussbaum claims that the person experiencing compassion must consider the suffering of the other as a significant part of his own scheme of goals and ends, an end whose good is to be promoted.[299] I think here she rightly points out that a person with his experiences gradually learns that others are an important part in his scheme of goals and ends. I am tempted to extend this principle further: When a child sees his parents, teachers being sensitive and helpful to other beings, they act like role models to him and he tries to copy them. Through this, he gradually learns compassion. He also learns it through rewards and punishments. Parents who teach compassion, reward for compassionate behavior and punish children when instances of imperviousness and cruelty are observed. In the same manner, religion and the stories which we grow up with teach compassion by way of role-modeling. Gradually, with what we have been taught, the conception of unconditional love is formed. Eventually it becomes our form of life. So this conditioning helps us develop a social understanding about things around us, and hence helps us to connect to each other in a way that makes compassion possible.

To sum up we can say that the analysis of the nature of compassion in different philosophical traditions shows that there is no one universal understanding of compassion. Although some share a common understanding on some points, yet they differ on others. In conclusion, this research leads us to conclude that compassion can be defined as a fellow-feeling arisen by the sight of suffering, which is in some manner innate, but mainly developed or learnt in one's form of life. Much more needs to be done on the nature of compassion. However I hope this research is beneficial to future researchers who wish to explore the subject.

Bibliography

1. Aristotle. *Rhetoric,* In *The Works of Aristotle,* ed. W. D. Ross. Oxford: Clarendon Press, 1968.
2. Aquinas, Thomas. *Summa Theologia*, edited by R. J. Batten. vol. 34. New York: McGraw-Hill Book Company; London: Eyre and Spottiwods, 1964.
3. Aquinas, Thomas. *Summa Theologia*, translated by The Fathers of English Dominican Province. Westminsters: Christian Classics, 1981. [book-on-line] available from http://www.library.du.ac.in/dspace/pdf ; Internet; accessed 21/05/2012, 390.
4. Barad, Judith. "The Understanding and Experience of Compassion: Aquinas and the Dalai Lama". *Buddhist-Christian Studies* 27, (2007). [Journal on-line]; available from http://www.jstor.org/page/info/about/policies/items.jsp; Internet; accessed 29/09/2011, 24.
5. Bhai Bala ji. *Sri Guru Nanak Dev Ji ki Janam Sakhi.* Amritsar: Bhai Chater Singh Jivan Singh Publication, 2008.
6. Buddhaghoṣa, Bhadantacariya. *Visuddhimagga*, translated by Bhikkhu Nanamoli. Colombo: Samayawardana Printers, 1991, [book on-line]; available from http://

www.accesstoinsight.org/lib/authors/nanamoli/Pathof Purification2011.pdf; Internet; accessed 31 October 2011.

7. Blum, Lawrence. "*Compassion*". In *Explaining Emotion,* edited by Amelie Oksenberg Rorty. London: University of California Press, 1980.

8. Brown, Lessley. *The New Shorter Oxford English Dictionary on Historical Principles.* Oxford: Clarendon, 2002. [on-line] available from ISBN-19-861271-0; Internet; accessed 15/06/2011.

9. Carr, Brian. "Pity and Compassion as Social Virtues". *Philosophy* 74, (1999). available from http://www.jstor.org/page/info/about/policies/items.jsp; Internet; accessed 29/09/2011, 411-429.

10. Cavanagh, E. Michael. "Rediscovering Compassion". *Journal of Religion and Health,* Vol. 34, No. 4, Winter, 1995. [Journal on-line], available from http://www.jstor.org/page/info/about/policies/items.jsp; Internet; accessed 26/12/2011.

11. Coe, Kathryn. "An Essay on the Origin of Compassion and Altruism". [article on-line], available from http://www.metanexus.net/archive/conference2003/pdf/WOLpaper_Coe_kathayn.pdf; Internet: accessed 09/07/2011.

12. *Dhammapada,* trans. Ven. Weragoda S. Thero. [book on-line], available from http://www.Buddhanet.net/pdf_file/damapada.pdf; Internet; accessed 20/12/2011, 1155.

13. Fortenbaugh, W. W. *Aristotle on Emotion: A Contribution to Philosophical, Psychological, Rhetoric, Poetics and Ethics.* London: Duckworth, 1975.

14. Harris, J. Elizabeth. "Detachment and Compassion in Early Buddhism". [Article on-line] available from http://www.accesstoinsight.org/lib/authors/haris/b141.html; Internet; accessed 3 October 2011.

15. Harvey, Aronson. *Love and Sympathy in Theravada Buddhism*. Delhi: Motilal Banarsidass Publication, 1999.

16. Harvey, Peter. *An Introduction to Buddhist Ethics.* United Kingdom: Cambridge University Press, 2000.

17. Hinsa S. Bhagat. *The Great Sikh Saints.* Delhi: National Book Shop, 1990.

18. Kaur, Satnaam. *Three Basic of Sikh Though: Faith, Grace and Prayers.* Delhi: Pragati Press, 1997.

19. Mcleod, H. W. *Sikh and Sikhism*. Oxford: Oxford University Press, 1999.

20. Nussbaum, Martha. *Upheavals of Thought; The Intelligence of Emotions.* London: Cambridge University Press, 2001.

21. *Oxford English Dictionary.* Edited by Angus Stevenson. 11th edition. Oxford: Clarendon Press, 2008.

21. Pence, E. Gregory. "Can Compassion be Taught?". *Journal of Medical Ethics*, Vol. 9, No. 4 (1983). [Journal on-line]; available from http://www.jstor.org/page/info/about/policies/items.jsp; Internet; accessed 17/08/2011.

22. Schopenhauer, Arthur. *On the Basis of Morality*, translated by E. F. J. Payne. Indianapolis: Bobbs-Merrill, 1965.

23. Singh, P. Bagat. "dAya". [article on-line] available from http://www.sikhphilosphy.net/spritual-article/27189_daya_print_pdf; Internet; accessed 15/05/2011.

24. Singh, Avtar. *Ethics of the Sikhs*. Patiala: Publication Eureau, 1983.

25. Singh, Harbans. *Guru Nanak and Origins of the Sikh faith*. India: Asia Publication House, 1969.

26. *Siri Guru Granth* Sahib, translated by Singh Sahib Sant Singh Kalsa, 3rd edition. Arizona: Hand made Books. [Book-online]: available from http://www.gurbanifiles.org/translations/English%20translation%20of20siri%20Guru%20Granth%20sahib.pdf ; Internet; accessed 7/02/2012, 249, 991, 1027, 727.

27. Snow E. Nancy, "Compassion". *American Philosophical Quarterly,* Vol. 28, No. 3 (Jul., 1991). [Journal on-line]; available from http://www.jstor.org/page/info/about/policies/items.jsp; Internet; accessed 26/08/2011.

28. Taylor, C. "Sympathy". *The Journal of Ethics*. vol. 3, No. 1 (1999). [Journal on-line], available from http://www.jstor.org/page/info/about/policies/items.jsp; Internet; accessed 23/10/2012.

References

1 *Siri Guru Granth* Sahib, trans. Singh Sahib Sant Singh Kalsa, 3rd ed. (Arizona: Hand made Books) [Book-online]: available from http://www.gurbanifiles.org/translations/English%20translation%20of20siri%20Guru%20Granth%20sahib.pdf ; Internet; accessed 7/02/2012, 1329.

2 Peter Harvey, *An Introduction to Buddhist Ethics*, (United Kingdom: Cambridge University Press, 2000), 104.

3 *Siri Guru Granth* Sahib, trans. Singh Sahib Sant Singh Kalsa, 3rd ed. (Arizona: Hand Made Books) [Book-online]: available from http://www.gurbanifiles.org/translations/English%20translation%20of20siri%20Guru%20Granth%20sahib.pdf ; Internet; accessed 7/02/2012, 2.

4 Kathryn Coe, "An Essay on the Origin of Compassion and Altruism", [article on-line], available from http://www.metanexus.net/archive/conference2003/pdf/WOLpaper_Coe_kathayn.pdf; Internet: accessed 09/07/2011, 6.

5 Arthur Schopenhauer, *On the Basis of Morality*, trans. E.F.J.Payne, (Indianapolis: Bobbs-Merrill, 1965), 145.

6 Martha Nussbaum, *Upheavals of Thought; The Intelligence of Emotions*, (London: Cambridge University Press, 2001), 320-321.

7 Compassion is not restricted only to human beings, but it also extends towards other entities (such as animals, tree etc.). But this is out of the preview of this dissertation.

8 Aristotle, *Rhetoric*, In *The Works of Aristotle*, ed. W.D.Ross, (Oxford: Clarendon press, 1968), 1385b12.

9 For a detail discussion see chapter 3.

10 Martha Nussbaum, *Upheavals of Thought; The Intelligence of Emotions*, (London: Cambridge University Press, 2001), 311.

11 Lawrence Blum, "Compassion," In *Explaining Emotion,* eds Amelie Oksenberg Rorty, (London: University of California Press, 1980), 508.

12 Carr, "Pity and Compassion as Social Virtues;" *Philosophy* 74, (1999), available from http://www.jstor.org/page/info/about/policies/items.jsp; Internet; accessed 29/09/2011, 420.

13 Martha Nussbaum, *Upheavals of Thought; The Intelligence of Emotions*,, 309.

14 As maintained by Lawrence Blum. Blum, "Compassion," 509-511.

15 Carr, "Pity and Compassion as Social Virtues," 420-421. For a detail discussion see chapter 2.

16 As according to Aristotle and Nancy E. Snow. Aristotle, *Rhetoric,* 1385b12; Nancy E. Snow, "Compassion," *American Philosophical Quarterly,* Vol. 28, No. 3 (Jul., 1991), [Journal on-line]; available from http://www.jstor.org/page/info/about/policies/items.jsp; Internet; accessed 26/08/2011,

17 Lawrence Blum, "Compassion," In *Explaining Emotion,* eds Amelie Oksenberg Rorty, (London: University of California Press, 1980).

18 Arthur Schopenhauer, *On the Basis of Morality*, trans. E.F.J.Payne, (Indianapolis: Bobbs-Merrill, 1965), 145.

19 C. Taylor, "Sympathy", *The Journal of Ethics*, vol. 3, No. 1 (1999), [Journal on-line], available from http://www.jstor.org/page/info/about/policies/items.jsp; Internet; accessed 23/10/1012.

20 Aronson B. Harvey, *Love and Sympathy in Theravāda Buddhism.* (Delhi: Motilal Banarsidass Publication, 1999).

21 Peter Harvey, *An Introduction to Buddhist Ethics*, (United Kingdom: Cambridge University Press, 2000).

22 Satnaam Kaur, *Three Basic of Sikh Though: Faith, Grace and Prayers*, (Delhi: Pragati Press, 1997), 100.

23 This is my own example.

24 Brown, Lessley, The New shorter Oxford English dictionary on historical principles, (Oxford: Clarendon, 2002), [on-line] available from ISBN-19-861271-0; Internet; accessed 15/06/2011.

25 Oxford English dictionary (2008).

26 Emphasis is mine.

27 Emphasis is mine.

28 Nancy E. Snow, "Compassion," *American Philosophical Quarterly,* Vol. 28, No. 3 (Jul., 1991), [Journal on-line]; available from http://www.jstor.org/page/info/about/policies/items.jsp; Internet; accessed 26/08/2011, 195.

29 Ibid.

30 Gregory E. Pence, "Can Compassion be Taught?," *Journal of Medical Ethics*, Vol. 9, No. 4 (1983), [Journal on-line]; available from http://www.jstor.org/page/info/about/policies/items.jsp; Internet; accessed 17/08/2011, 189-191.

31 Brian Carr, "Pity and Compassion as Social Virtues," *Philosophy* 74, (1999), available from http://www.jstor.org/page/info/about/policies/items.jsp; Internet; accessed 29/09/2011, 411-429.

32 Lawrence Blum, "Compassion," In *Explaining Emotion,* eds Amelie Oksenberg Rorty, (London: University of California Press, 1980), 508.

33 Snow, "Compassion", 197.

34 Blum, "Compassion," 508.

35 Nussbaum, *Upheavals of Thought; The Intelligence of Emotions*, 307.

36 Snow, "Compassion," 197.

37 Ibid., 195.

38 It is a debatable issues that whether compassion includes sorrow or not. For the sake of non-deviation from the current topic I will explain this issue in later chapters.

39 Snow, "Compassion," 197.

40 Pence, "Can Compassion be Taught?," 189.

41 Snow, "Compassion," 196.

42 Blum, "Compassion," 512

43 Ibid.

44 Snow, "Compassion," 196.

45 Carr, "Pity and Compassion as Social Virtues", 420. For a detail discussion see chapter2.

46 Ibid.

47 Ibid.

48 Snow, "Compassion," p. 197.

49 Ibid.

50 Ibid., 197-198; Blum, "Compassion", 510.

51 Snow, "Compassion," p. 195.

52 Ibid.

53 Aristotle, *Rhetoric,* In *The Works of Aristotle,* ed. W.D.Ross, (Oxford: Clarendon Press, 1968), 1385b12-1386b8.

54 Blum, "Compassion," p. 509.

55 Ibid.

56 Ibid., 510.

57 Blum, "Compassion," 510.

58 Pence, "Can compassion be taught?," 189.

59 Blum, "Compassion," 510.

60 Carr, "Pity and Compassion as Social Virtues," 421.

61 Ibid., 421-422.

62 Pence, "Can Compassion be Taught?," 189.

63 Ibid.

64 Ibid., 189.

65 Snow, "Compassion," 199.

66 Ibid.

67 Nussbaum, *Upheavals of Thought; The Intelligence of Emotions*, 320-321.

68 Snow, "Compassion," p. 197.

69 Ibid.

70 Emphasis is mine.

71 This historical account is purely based on the analysis made by Nussbaum in sixth chapter of her book. Martha Nussbaum, *Upheavals of Thought; The Intelligence of Emotions*, (London: Cambridge University Press, 2001), 303.

72 *Eleos* sometimes translated as pity, but I have followed Martha Nussbaum in avoiding that term partly because of its contemporary connotations of condescension. Nussbaum asserts that "pity" has recently come to have nuances of condescension and superiority to the sufferer that it did not have when Rousseau invoked *pitie,* and still does not have when "pity" is used to translate the Greek tragic terms *eleos* and *oiktos.* Nussbaum, *Upheavals of Thought; The Intelligence of Emotions*, 301.

73 Aristotle, *Rhetoric,* In *The Works of Aristotle,* ed. W.D.Ross, (Oxford: Clarendon press, 1968), 1385b12

74 According to Aristotle, 'emotions are all those feelings that so change men as to affect their judgments, and that are also attended by pain or pleasure. Such as anger, pity, fear and the like, with their opposites'. Rhetoric, 1378a20

75 Ibid., 1378a24.

76 Ibid., 1378a25.

77 Ibid., 1378a25-26.

78 Ibid., 1378a27-28.

79 Ibid., 1386a5.

80 Ibid., 1386a9.

81 Ibid., 1386a6-8.

82 Ibid., 1386a8-12.

83 I have reformulated this example. The original example of Aristotle was 'the arrival of the great king's gift for Diopeithes after his death'. I reformulated this as the identity of this man is not clear from the sources?

84 Ibid., 1386a12-13.

85 Ibid., 1385b35-36.

86 Ibid., 1386a16-17.

87 Ibid., 1386a24-26.

88 Ibid., 1386a25-31.

89 Ibid., 1386a28-30.

90 Ibid., 1386a23-24.

91 Ibid., 1386a26-28.

92 Ibid., 1385b24-26.

93 Ibid., 1385b26.

94 Ibid., 1385b27.

95 Ibid., 1385b27-28.

96 Ibid., 1385b28-29.

97 Ibid., 1385a19-21.

98 Ibid., 1385a23.

99 Ibid., 1385a18-19.

100 This example is self-expounded.

101 Ibid., 1385b9-24, 31-2.

102 Ibid., 1385b34-35.

103 Ibid.

104 This could get us into a controversy deviating could us from the present discussion, so without getting into the details, it is worthwhile to keep in mind that, for Aristotle a noble person is the one who always performs noble deeds. His deeds define his nobility.

105 See page 35-36.

106 Thomas Aquinas, *Summa Theologia,* trans. The Fathers of English Dominican Province, (Westminsters: Christian Classics, 1981) [book-on-line] available from http://www.library.du.ac.in/dspace/pdf ; Internet; accessed 21/05/2012, 390.

107 Thomas Aquinas, *Summa Theologia,* ed.R.J.Batten, vol. 34 (New York: McGraw-hill Book Company; London: Eyre and Spottiwods, 1964), 209.

108 Ibid., 209.

109 Ibid., 211.

110 Ibid., 211.

111 Thomas Aquinas, *Summa Theologia,* (1981), 390.

112 Ibid., 390.

113 Ibid., 373.

114 Thomas Aquinas, *Summa Theologia,* (1964), 209.

115 Dr. Robert Stackpole, *St. Thomas Aquinas on the Virtue of Mercy,* 1.

116 Ibid.

117 Ibid.

118 Thomas Aquinas, *Summa Theologia,* (1981), p. 392.

119 Ibid.

120 Ibid., 392.

121 Ibid., 392-93.

122 Judith Barad, "The Understanding and Experience of Compassion: Aquinas and the Dalai Lama", Buddhist-Christian Studies 27, (2007), [Journal on-line]; available from http://www.jstor.org/page/info/about/policies/items.jsp; Internet; accessed 29/09/2011, 24.

123 Ibid.

124 Thomas Aquinas, *Summa Theologia,* (1964), 217.

125 Ibid., 221.

126 As he defined above.

127 To make this point clearer Nussbaum cited examples given in Candacc Clark's study. According to Clark, Americans today tend to include more relatively mild predicaments in the list of plights than they did formerly. Nussbaum, *Upheavals of Thought; The Intelligence of Emotions*, 307-308.

128 Ibid., 207.

129 Ibid., 309-10.

130 Ibid., 309.

131 Ibid.

132 Ibid.

133 Ibid.

134 Ibid., 311.

135 Ibid., 311.

136 Ibid., p. 313.

137 Ibid., 314.

138 Ibid.

139 I raise these questions to compare Nussbaum's view with Buddhist's view. As according to Nussbaum, loss of valuable things causes suffering, while for Buddhist these so called valuable things itself are the cause of suffering. I will discuss this point further in next chapter.

140 Ibid., 318.

141 Ibid., 319.

142 Ibid., 320

143 Ibid.

144 Ibid.

145 Ibid., 320-321

146 Ibid.

147 Ibid., 321.

148 Brian Carr, "Pity and Compassion as Social Virtues," *Philosophy* 74, (1999), available from http://www.jstor.org/page/info/about/policies/items.jsp; Internet; accessed 29/09/2011, 419.

149 Nussbaum, *Upheavals of Thought; The Intelligence of Emotions*, 321.

150 Carr, "Pity and Compassion as Social Virtues," 415-416.

151 Ibid., 414.

152 Ibid.

153 Ibid.

154 Ibid., 411.

155 These examples have been discussed in the previous section.

156 Carr, "Pity and Compassion as Social Virtues," 420.

157 Ibid., 421

158 Ibid., 420.

159 Ibid.

160 Ibid.

161 Ibid.

162 Ibid., 420-23.

163 Ibid., 421.

164 Ibid., 423.

165 Ibid., 421-22.

166 Ibid., 422.

167 Ibid., 423.

168 See page 32.

169 Nussbaum, *Upheavals of Thought; The Intelligence of Emotions*, 314.

170 Carr, "Pity and Compassion as Social Virtues," 423.

171 Carr, "Pity and Compassion as Social Virtues," 423.

172 Ibid.

173 Aristotle, in *Rhetoric*, defines compassion as an emotion. In the *Nicomachean Ethics* also, Aristotle does consider it as an emotion along with a host of others: 'appetite, anger, fear ....envy, joy, friendly feeling, hatred ... and in general the feelings that are accompanied by pleasure or pain. Aristotle, *Rhetoric*, 1385b; idem., *Nicomachean Ethics*, 1105b21.

174 Nussbaum, *Upheavals of Thoughts; The Intelligence of Emotions*, 301.

175 Carr, "Pity and Compassion as Social Virtues," 401.

176 Gregory E. Pence, "Can Compassion be Taught?," *Journal of Medical Ethics*, Vol. 9, No. 4 (1983), [Journal on-line]; available from http://www.jstor.org/page/info/about/policies/items.jsp; Internet; accessed 17/08/2011, 189.

177 Thomas Aquinas, *Summa Theologia*, (1981), 394-97.

178 W.W. Fortenbaugh, *Aristotle on Emotion: A Contribution to Philosophical, Psychological, Rhetoric, Poetics and Ethics*, (London: Duckworth, 1975), 79.

179 Ibid., 80.

180 Ibid.

181 Ibid., 83.

182 These differences are also cited by Carr. Carr, "Pity and Compassion as Social Virtues", 416-418.

183 Aristotle, *Nicomachean Ethics*, 1105b31-1106a2.

184 Ibid.

185 Aristotle, *Nicomachean Ethics*, 1106a3-4.

186 Aristotle, *Nicomachean Ethics*, 1106b15-24.

187 As also discussed above.

188 As according to her a compassionate-feeler judges the seriousness of suffering and also the object on whom he is going to feel compassion. As discussed above.

189 *Visuddhimagga* (*Pāli*; English *The Path of Purification*) is a Theravāda Buddhist commentary written by Buddhaghoṣa approximately in 430 CE in Sri Lanka. It is an encyclopedic and masterful summary and exposition of the teaching of the Theravāda Buddhism, as it was understood by the elders of the *Mahavihara* Monastery in Anuradhapura, Sri Lanka. It is considered the most important Theravāda text outside of the *Tipitaka* Canon of scriptures.

190 Harvey B. Aronson, *Love and Sympathy in Theravāda Buddhism*, (Delhi: Motilal Banarsidass Publication, 1999), 3.

191 Ibid.

192 Bhadantacariya Buddhaghoṣa, *Visuddhimagga*, trans. Bhikkhu Ñāṇamoli, (Colombo: Samayawardana printers, 1991), [book on-line]; available from http://www.accesstoinsight.org/lib/authors/nanamoli/Pathof Purification2011.pdf; Internet; accessed 31 October 2011, 371.

193 For the sake of continuity, I will latter discuss this difference in detail.

194 Aronson, *Love and Sympathy in Theravāda Buddhism*, 16.

195 Ibid., 1.

196 Ibid.

197 Ibid.

198 *Brahmavihāra*, which in Ṣanskrit means "living in the Brahman-heaven", is the four noble practices of mental development. It is believed that through these mental development men can attain subsequent rebirth in the Brahman-world. In the *Pāli* canon, the Buddha recommends cultivating these four virtuous practices to both householders and monastics. These four practices are: (1) *mettā*; Sanskrit: *maitrī*, (2) *karuṇā*, (3) *muditā*, (4) *upekkha*; Sanskrit: *upekṣa*. *Mettā* is a perfect virtue of love and kindness, which gives happiness to all living beings; *karuṇā* is a perfect virtue of compassion, which removes pain from living beings; *muditā* is a perfect virtue of joy, the enjoyment of the sight of others who have attained happiness; *Upekṣa* is a perfect virtue of equanimity, being free from attachment to everything and being indifferent to living beings. These four are also known as *apramāGas* (infinite feelings), because these practices give happiness to infinite living beings.

199 Bhadantacariya Buddhaghoṣa, *Visuddhimagga*, 371.

200 *Dhammapada*, trans. Ven. Weragoda S. Thero, http://www.Buddhanet.net/pdf_file/damapada.pdf; Internet; accessed 20/12/2011, 1155.

201 Aronson, *Love and Sympathy in Theravāda Buddhism*, 63.

202 Ibid.

203 *Mettā* is defined as the sincere wish for the welfare and genuine happiness of all living beings without exception. It is genuine feeling of love, which is not necessary based on sight of suffering.

204 These questions are self-expounded.

205 Buddhaghoṣa, *Visuddhimagga*, 372.

206 Ibid.

207 Aristotle defined compassion as a sorrow or pain. See chapter 2.

208 Aronson, *Love and Sympathy in Theravāda Buddhism*, 65.

209 Ibid.

210 Dhammapada, 441.

211 Meaning of the second one is more appropriate for Buddhist.

212 Elizabeth J. Harris, "Detachment and Compassion in Early Buddhism," [Article on-line] available from http://www.accesstoinsight.org/lib/authors/haris/b141.html; Internet; accessed 3 October 2011. 2.

213 *Dhammapada*, 443.

214 *Mettā* is the first of the four sublime states. It is defined as the sincere

wish for the welfare and genuine happiness of all living beings without exception. It is also explained as the friendly disposition, for a genuine friend sincerely wishes for the welfare of his friend. *Mettā* is neither carnal love nor personal affection. *Mettā* enables one to regard all as fellow beings. In other words, it is extended even towards one's foe and enemy.

215 Aronson, *Love and Sympathy in Theravāda Buddhism*, 6.

216 Ibid., 7.

217 Buddhaghoṣa, *Visuddhimagga*, 372.

218 Ibid., 373.

219 Ibid., 373.

220 Aronson, *Love and Sympathy in Theravāda Buddhism*, 16.

221 Ibid.

222 Ibid.

223 Ibid., 13.

224 Ibid., 64.

225 Ibid.

226 Buddhaghoṣa, *Visuddhimagga*, 365.

227 Buddhaghoṣa, *Visuddhimagga*, 366.

228 From this, I think, one should not conclude that Buddhism is against punishment. Buddhism is not against punishment of wrong deeds. As they believe that a wrong deed of one is an injustice towards another being, and not opposing act of injustice means becoming part of it. Buddhists makes a distinction between a wrong doer and his wrong deed. They believe that a wrong doer is a subject of compassion and his action is to be opposed. In nut-shell they believe in retributive form of punishment, for which compassion is a necessary element.

229 "For this is the escape from ill will, friends, that is to say, the mind-deliverance of loving-kindness.... For this is the escape from cruelty, friends, that is to say, the mind-deliverance of compassion... for this is the escape from boredom, friends, that is to say, the mind-deliverance of gladness... for this is the escape from greed, friends, that is to say, the mind-deliverance of equanimity"; Buddhaghoṣa, *Visuddhimagga*, 370

230 Ibid.

231 If from a brahman's family... if from a merchant's family... if from a worker's family... and if from whatever family he has gone forth from

home into homelessness and has come into this *dhamma* and discipline taught by the *Tathaagata*, having thus developed friendliness (*mettā*), compassion (*karuṇā*), sympathetic joy (*mudita*), and equanimity (*upekkha*), he attains inward calm — I say it is by inward calm that he is following the practices suitable for recluses.

232 Here 'excellent existence' means a stage of liberation.

233 Bagat Puran Singh, "Daya", [article on-line] available from http://www.sikhphilosphy.net/spritual-article/27189_daya_print_pdf ; Internet; accessed 15/05/2011,1.

234 Ibid.

235 In Ādi Granth, *mahadaial* (super compassionate), *Daial puruk, daiapati* (lord of compassion), *daial dev* (merciful god), *karima, rahima* (the merciful one), etc., have been used as attributive names of God. *Siri Guru Granth* Sahib, trans. Singh Sahib Sant Singh Kalsa, 3rd ed. (Arizona: Hand made Books) [Book-online]: available from http://www.gurbanifiles.org/translations/English%20translation%20of20siri%20Guru%20Granth%20sahib.pdf ; Internet; accessed 7/02/2012, 249, 991, 1027, 727.

236 Satnaam Kaur, *Three Basic of Sikh Though: Faith, Grace and Prayers*, (Delhi: Pragati Press, 1997), 100.

237 Ibid.

238 Ibid.

239 The primary scripture of the Sikhs is variously referred to as the *Granth Sahib*, the *Guru Granth Sahib*, the Ādi Granth, or as an expanded combination of the latter two. Here, *Granth* simply means a book. And to this the Honorific *Sahib* is supplemented to designate Sanctity. The *Guru* is merely prefixed as an indication of the status of *Guru* as now attached to this particular scripture. And the alternative title Ādi Granth (where 'Ādi' means 'first' or 'original') is used to distinguish the first scripture of the Sikhs from *Dasam Granth*, ascribed to the tenth *Guru, Guru Granth Sahib*. W.H.Mcleod, *Sikh and* Sikhism, (Oxford: Oxford University Press, 1999), 59.

240 Arjan Dev was the fifth *Guru* of Sikhs.

241 Avtar Singh, *Ethics of the Sikhs*, (Patiala: Publication Eureau, 1983), 1, 8.

242 Ibid., 11.

243 Ibid., 10.

244 W.H.Mcleod, *Sikh and* Sikhism, 8.

245 Ibid., 9.

246 Ibid.

247 Avtar Singh, *Ethics of the Sikhs*, P. 13.

248 Ibid.

249 Ibid.

250 Ibid., 2-3.

251 Guru Nanak is the founder of Sikhism and is the first of the ten Sikh Gurus of the Sikhs.

252 I have translated this from the following Punjabi text. Bhai Bala ji, Sri Guru Nanak Dev Ji ki Janam Sākhi, (Amritsar: Bhai Chater Singh Jivan Singh Publication, 2008), 105. Harbans Singh, *Guru Nanak and Origins of the Sikh faith*, (India: Asia Publication House, 1969), 84.

253 Bhai kahaniya ji was born in 1648 A.D. in Wazirabad (now in Pakistan). He was a firm believer of Guru's teaching.

254 They were especially annoyed because the city had been surrounded; stopping the supply of food and water, and here was Bhai Kanhaiya sharing what little water they had.

255 *Siri Guru Granth Sahib*, 922.

256 *Siri Guru Granth Sahib*, 1299.

257 Bhagat Singh Hinsa, *The Great Sikh Saints*, (Delhi: National Book Shop, 1990), 36-37.

258 In Sikh ethics, universal brotherhood is an important tenet of equality. It is said that all people emanate from the same spiritual continuum and to the same ultimate source they will all be returning. The whole of humanity is bound by a fraternal relationship. Avtar Singh, *Ethics of the Sikhs*, p. 184.

259 See chapter 2.

260 For details see chapter 2.

261 Avtar Singh, *Ethics of the Sikhs*, 184.

262 Every person who believes in Sikhism is required to work and pray for this universal brotherhood by praying for and seeking the good of all which is described in Sikhism as *sarbaht da bhala*.

263 In Ādi Granth compassion is described as a virtue, as following saying asserts: "Pilgrimages, austere discipline, compassion and charity – these, by themselves, bring an iota of merit. Listening and believing with

love and humility in your mind, cleanse yourself with the name, at the sacred shrine deep within. All virtues are your, Lord, I have none at all. Without virtue, there is no devotional worship". *Siri Guru Granth Sahib*, 4.

264 Ibid., 3.

265 Ibid., 903.

266 Ibid., 340.

267 Ibid., 793.

268 Ibid., 351.

269 Avtar Singh, *Ethics of the Sikhs*, 190.

270 *Siri Guru Granth Sahib*, 356.

271 Ibid., 1169.

272 Avtar Singh, *Ethics of the Sikhs*, p. 85.

273 Guru Teghbhadur was the ninth Guru of Sikh religion who stood against Aurangzeb atrocious policies for conversion of hindus (Kasmiri Pandit) to Islam. He (Guru Tegh Bahadur) laid down the gauntlet in the fight for freedom of religion and told the Pandits to inform Aurangzeb that the Brahmins would gladly accept and embrace Islam if Guru Tegh Bahadur can be convinced to do so.

274 Ibid.

275 *Siri Guru Granth Sahib*, 1101.

276 Ibid., 966.

277 Ibid., 822.

278 Ibid., 1152.

279 Ibid., 85.

280 Ibid., 414.

281 Ibid., 766.

282 Nussbaum, *Upheavals of Thought; The Intelligence of Emotions*, 309-10.

283 Ibid., 309.

284 Ibid.

285 Brian Carr, "Pity and Compassion as Social Virtues," *Philosophy* 74, (1999), available from http://www.jstor.org/page/info/about/policies/items.jsp; Internet; accessed 29/09/2011, 423.

286 Ibid.

287 For detail discussion see chapter 2.

288 Nussbaum, *Upheavals of Thought; The Intelligence of Emotions*, 307.

289 This discussion was tackled in the second chapter.

290 Carr, "Pity and Compassion as Social Virtues," 420

291 Carr's notion of felt suffering is defined in the chapter 2.

292 A more detailed discussion is given in chapter 2.

293 For detail discussion see chapter 2.

294 Carr, "Pity and Compassion as Social Virtues," 423.

295 For details see chapter 2.

296 For detail see chapter2.

297 Nussbaum named it as desert requirement. See chapter-2.

298 For detail see chapter 2.

299 For detail see chapter 2.

Index

A

A selfless act 60
Ability to identify 26
Actual suffering 28
Affection 15
Affectionate devotion 15, 19
Altruistic behavior 9, 15
Altruistic emotion 40
Attachment 15, 19, 32
Austerities 73

B

Beliefs 16
Benevolence 14, 80
Biblical tradition 2
Blame-worthiness 13
Blamelessness 35
Bodily sensations 45
Brahma gods 55
Buddhism 1, 6, 8, 15, 20, 49, 58, 61, 76, 78, 79, 80, 81, 82, 83
Buddhist discourses 50, 56
Buddhist ethics 7
Buddhist teachings 49, 51
Buddhist understandings 6

C

Capability of remembrance 48
Capability of supposing 32
Christianity 1
Cognitive elements 39
Compassion 50, 73, 80
Compassionate-feeler 3
Compassionate-object 19
Complexities 28
Courageous emotion 27, 46
Culpable actions 43
Cultivating minds 52

D

Danger of suffering 31
Deliverance of mind 60
Destructive emotions 60
Dharmic faith 73
Directed behavior 46
Discomfort 11
Discrimination 78
Divine abiding 61

E

Earned suffering 28
Emotion 10, 24, 27, 28, 62, 82
Emotional attitude 2
Emotional distance 14
Emotional reaction 11
Empathy 10
Ephemeral feeling 31
Epistemological requirement 38
Eudaimonistic imagination 39
Eudaimonistic judgment 19, 33, 37, 40, 48, 83, 86
Eudemonistic requirement 33, 37
Evaluative judgment 47
Evil caused by luck 24
Evil fortune 25
Expression of sympathy 50
External suffering 27

F

Felt suffering 76
Fraternal activity 57
Friendlessness 24

G

Generosity 9
God's force 7
Gotama Buddha 50
Gurbani 67
Gurmukhi 64
Guru Arjan Dev 63
Guru Gobind Singh 66
Guru Granth Sahib 63, 69
Guru Nanak 65, 66, 70, 73
Guru Teghbhadur 72
Guru's qualities 75

H

Heartfelt sympathy 30
Heartfelt-sympathy 32
Hindrance of attachment 54
Human flourishing 37
Human instinct 4
Human interactions 1
Human suffering 39

I

Identity confusion 16
Imagination 16, 17, 19, 20, 21, 38, 48
Imagination of object conditions 15
Imaginative abilities 19
Imaginative dwelling 3
Imaginative reconstruction 17
India 75
Indian philosophical traditions 1
Intellectual imaginative reconstruction 17
Internal cognitive elements 27
Interpersonal attraction 15
Interpersonal distance 12
Involve cognition 45

J

Judgment 82
Judgment of non-desertion 39
Judgment of size 39

K

Kasmiri pandits 72

L

Lack of understanding 38
Level of concentration 50
Liberating action 60
Loving-kindness 52, 60

M

Measureless state 61
Meditation 55, 56, 57, 58, 61, 62, 73
Meditative cultivation 51
Meditative development 56, 79
Miserable heart 29
Misfortunate condition 38
Misfortune 12, 18, 19, 25, 26, 37, 38
Moral systems 9
Moral values 6

N

Non-practical emotion 45, 46
Non-serious suffering 4

O

Our-own vulnerability 32
Overpowering evil 30
Own sufferings 59
Own vulnerability 18, 20

P

Painful emotion 27, 28
Painful things 24
Personal judgments 85
Philosophical traditions 87
Powerful emotion 15
Powerful imagination 18
Practical emotions 45
Predicament of adolescence 36
Puzzling nature 9

R

Rape victims 2
Rational desire 33
Recognition 21, 26, 32
Recognition of our own vulnerability 15
Relationships 1, 3
Religious declarations 65

S

Sacha Soda 65
Scarcity of friends 24
self-centered emotion 39
Self-discipline 73
Self-sacrifice 9
Self-sufficient 27
Self-transposal 17
Sense of superiority 13
Sensibility towards 52
Serious suffering 4, 24, 83
Seriousness of suffering 3
Shared vulnerability 38
Sight of suffering 51
Sikh ethics 7
Sikh ideology 65
Sikh literatures 63
Sikh Religious Thought 62
Sikhism 1, 7, 8, 15, 20, 49, 62, 64, 68, 71, 76, 77, 78, 79, 80, 81, 82, 83
Simple compassion 50
Social interconnection 1
Social relationships 7

Social standing 25
Strong imagination 17
Subject's judgment 16
Subject's reaction 51
Suffering 6, 10, 11, 12, 13, 15, 18, 24, 25-28, 30, 31, 35, 39, 41, 43, 50-53, 55, 60, 61, 62, 68, 78, 83, 84, 85
Suffering people 29
Symbol of heartlessness 53
Sympathetic response 3
Sympathy 6, 10, 11, 12, 14, 20, 22, 50, 80

T

Terrorists' attacks 2
Theravada Buddhism 50
Theravada Buddhist 6, 49
Theravada tradition 54
Tragedies of modern life 28
Types of emotions 45

U

Unconditional love 54, 55, 78, 83
Undeniable dangers 43
Unfelt suffering 41, 84
Universal understanding 82
Unlike pity 80

V

Victims of misfortune 16, 42
Violence 6
Volitional dimension 40
Vulnerabilities 3, 21, 26, 36

W

Warm affection 15, 19
Willingness to listen 18